D1053595

AS LONG AS WE BOTH SHALL LIVE

DR. GARY SMALLEY

Bestselling Author of *The Language of Love*

TED CUNNINGHAM

AS LONG AS
WE BOTH
SHALL LIVE

Experience the Marriage You've Always Wanted

Regal

From Gospel Light
Ventura, California, U.S.A.

Published by Regal
From Gospel Light
Ventura, California, U.S.A.
www.regalbooks.com
Printed in the U.S.A.

Library of Congress Cataloging-in-Publication Data
Smalley, Gary.
As long as we both shall live : experience the marriage you've always wanted /
Gary Smalley and Ted Cunningham.
p. cm.
ISBN 978-0-8307-4680-4 (hard cover)
1. Marriage—Religious aspects—Christianity. I. Cunningham, Ted. II. Title.
BV835.S5523 2009
248.8'44—dc22
2009033176

1 2 3 4 5 6 7 8 9 10 / 15 14 13 12 11 10 09

Rights for publishing this book outside the U.S.A. or in non-English languages are
administered by Gospel Light Worldwide, an international not-for-profit ministry.
For additional information, please visit www.glww.org, email info@glww.org, or write to
Gospel Light Worldwide, 1957 Eastman Avenue, Ventura, CA 93003, U.S.A.

I (Gary) dedicate this book to my incredible staff at the
Smalley Relationship Center. Each day I wake up amazed at how
God is using you to minister to couples around the world.
You are the reason this message is getting out.
Thank you!

I (Ted) dedicate this book to my two children.
Corynn Mae, your caring heart and prayers each night melt me.
Carson Matthew, you have such a great sense of humor and
heart for prayer. I am so proud of both of you! Your mom and I pray
daily for your future spouses that they, too, are learning the three
most important things in life: to honor God, to honor
others and to honor others' things.

CONTENTS

ACKNOWLEDGMENTS

Margaret Feinberg, you are the best! You are a gifted wordsmith and passionate writer. Your energy bleeds through on every page.

A big thank you to Alex Field. You have been so encouraging and a pure delight to work with. Thank you, Kim Bangs, for your devotion and hard work behind this project.

Thank you, Regal and Gospel Light! Bill Greig, you lead your team with excellence.

We also want to say thank you to all of the staff at the Smalley Relationship Center. Day in and day out you serve marriages around the world. Your hard work does not go unnoticed. Thank you.

Thank you, Norma Smalley, Terry Brown, Ron Cunningham, Bonnie Cunningham, Scott Weatherford, Kim Fertig, Sue Parks and Roger Gibson for reading the manuscript and offering great insight.

The staff at Woodland Hills Community Church played a big part in this book. Ted Burden offered many valuable teaching insights. Pam Strayer transcribed, and Denise Bevins handled so many details of my life during the process. Richard Williams helped with the creative process. Thank you! Thank you! Thank you!

To all of our family and friends, many of whom have stories that fill these pages, we love you and owe a debt of gratitude for your patience in this process.

PERSONAL NOTE FROM GARY

This is my third book with Ted Cunningham. I have known Ted and his wife, Amy, for eight years. He is a great husband and the father of two wonderful kids, Corynn and Carson. Not only is Ted my dear friend, and a great writer and communicator, but he is also my pastor.

Ted and I have served as elders together at Woodland Hills Church in Branson, Missouri, for more than five years now. Each week, my wife, Norma, and I are thrilled to see how God is using Ted to reach thousands in our community. His messages are so practical and vulnerable. I have learned much from Ted and have thoroughly enjoyed writing this book with him. I know you will learn much from him too.

The names of those mentioned throughout this book, as well as the details of the stories, have been changed to protect the identities as well as the relationships of those involved.

AS LONG AS
We Both
SHALL LIVE

GREAT EXPECTATIONS

The expectations you bring to marriage color what you give and what you get, in all aspects of the relationship. Knowing what your specific expectations are and knowing how to handle them will speed your satisfaction and chase away the double threat of disillusionment and disconnection. Just watch how a seemingly perfect marriage could be affected in a negative way by dashed expectations during one frightening event.

Athletic, good-looking and fun-loving, Jon was the kind of guy women dreamed of marrying. When he met Heather, he knew he had found the love of his life. The young couple enjoyed a storybook wedding, and their marriage was off to a great start. In their free time, they faithfully served together as volunteers with our youth group.

I (Ted) enjoyed watching this couple and their relationship grow together. I'll never forget the day I was fishing at Taneycomo Lake in Branson, Missouri, when to my surprise I looked up to see Jon and Heather in waders, fishing rods in hand. It blew me away. What could be more perfect than a couple that enjoyed fly-fishing together?

For their one-year anniversary, they took a trip out West. They spent the week in Wyoming, fly-fishing in a private stream, and stayed in a palatial home. It was a dream vacation.

On the first day of fishing, Heather headed down to the stream with Jon, her lover and best friend. It was a cool, clear morning. The backdrop of the mountains, the ripples in the stream and the solitude transformed this fishing trip into a wildly romantic getaway. This would be one of the most memorable days of Heather's life.

Jon wondered how things could get any better. He had a wife who loved the things he loved and made his dreams a reality. Looking at

Heather, he said a quiet prayer of thanks for his beautiful bride.

After a few hours of fishing, Jon and Heather began making their way down the stream to find a better spot. Rounding the corner, they found themselves face to face with a monstrous moose.

Rather than back down, the moose snorted loudly and took a step toward Jon and Heather. The couple looked for a quick exit but found the banks on either side of the stream high and covered in tall prairie grass. Well aware that moose will attack when they feel trapped, the young couple knew they were in a serious situation.[1]

Fearing for his life, Jon edged himself and Heather over to the side of the stream. Unfortunately, the bank was too high and awkward for them to climb. In a panic, Jon scurried up the side of the bank, clawing for any clump of prairie grass he could get his hands on. Heather distinctly remembers Jon elbowing her out of the way to get a head start. Her knight in shining armor left her alone to face a gigantic moose. If the animal attacked, she would have to face it on her own. Or at least that's how Heather tells the story.

Jon's version is slightly different. He emphatically denies elbowing Heather but admits he was indeed the first one out of the stream. Jon offers a clear and valiant explanation for his reaction; his plan was to get out of the stream, brace himself on top of the bank and reach down for Heather, pulling her out of the moose's way.

Needless to say, from Heather's perspective, her husband's reaction to the situation left her a bit disillusioned. Where was the brave man she had come to expect? Why did her knight in shining armor elbow her out of the way? What happened to the man that any woman would expect to lay down his life for her?

Expectations Are Common to All

Everyone walks into marriage with a set of expectations. These expectations are made up of ideas and concepts that have been planted in our minds and hearts through a wide variety of sources—from overly romanticized film stories and song lyrics to ideals and concepts gathered at school, within our family of origin and the lives of other couples we have known. All of these sources combine to give us an idea of what the perfect marriage should look like.

Some of these expectations are spoken, but the vast majority are unspoken yet embedded in our worldview. Whether you realized it or not, after you said "I do," you packed more than just clothes, toiletries and shoes in your luggage and headed off on your honeymoon. You brought along all of your thoughts of the future, your hopes for a future family and your dreams of romance.

Many of those hopes and dreams are not only good, but they're also healthy for a marriage. A desire for close companionship, deep and satisfying conversation, the intimacy and thrill of lovemaking, the birth of precious children and a comfortable home life are wonderful to think about and even better to experience! But what happens if some of those great expectations aren't met? What then?

For many couples, the perfect marriage includes a house. Lots of young couples get excited about their first home. They can imagine the cute three-bedroom, two-bath home where they can begin to raise a family. This will be a place where they can enjoy each other and live a happy life together.

After they move into their new home and do just a little renovation (which goes as speedily and smoothly as an episode of *Extreme Makeover Home Edition*), along will come the kids. Before they know it, they will have a three-year-old and a one-year-old. Life will be exhausting but good!

The years will roll by without heartache or pain. They look forward to the day when their first child enters high school and they'll be able to proudly exhibit a sticker on their minivan's bumper that reads "My child is an honor roll student." After all, their kids aren't just average—their report cards will be stacked with *A*s and *B*s.

Is this close to how you imagine life will be?

Your expectations may also include that your spouse will stay madly in love with you, and you'll come home to find your bath drawn with bubbles and a hot gourmet meal . . . or a surprise "whisked away" weekend on a regular basis. You won't know what to do with all the chocolate, flowers or intimate time for just the two of you. And your spouse is going to smell so good every night . . . and every morning.

After dinner, you'll sit down together—because you both are so into the relationship—and talk about how you can make your relationship even more exemplary. Time spent praying and studying the Bible together will be effortless. And you'll wrap up almost every night with romance.

If you're a guy, you have your own image of what your wife is going to be wearing that evening. You may think you'll be doing it 5, 10 or 15 times a week. And if you're a gal, you have your image of intimacy—what real connection feels like—all those moments of talking, discussing and communicating—before and after sex.

Life will be so-o-o-o good.

And of course, you'll have friends to play golf or shop with frequently. And the same schedule you used to have—Monday night with the guys or Tuesday night with the gals—will be easy to keep. You'll like the same people. You'll connect with the same couples. Finding friends who love the same things you and your spouse do will be a snap!

Few couples before marriage discuss any of these expectations because they just don't get around to it or they're afraid of embarrassment if their mate found out. And then you get married . . .

You may find that the mortgage for the house you really love is slightly outside of your price range. Conceiving a baby might be more difficult than you anticipated. And once you have a baby, life is still good but never the same. Bubble baths and gourmet dinners are a rare treat—not a daily standard. And growing spiritually together takes more intentionality than you ever anticipated. While sex may not be as frequent as you had imagined, neither is the time for real connection and communication after the daily duties of work, cooking, cleaning, paying bills and taking care of the lawn. And when you find a friend you really like, your spouse doesn't like your new friend's spouse.

Finally, you wake up one day and realize that many of the expectations you carried into your marriage aren't getting met. Married life wasn't supposed to be like this, and you don't know what to do about your disappointment.

That's what this book is all about. We want to help you move beyond any unhealthy or unrealistic expectations and into an abundant, life-giving marriage where your needs are met and your dreams are realized. But this kind of transformation doesn't happen overnight. That's why, in the upcoming pages, we are going to share stories from our own marriages as well as from the marriages of those we know and counsel. We have seen the discovery and application of the ideas we will describe in the upcoming chapters literally breathe life back into marriages that were dying. We have seen couples grow to new depths of understanding and love for each other. And we have seen their marital satisfaction skyrocket.

Through the years, we have witnessed the progression of many marriages start with unmet expectations that lead to disillusionment and disconnect, which can eventually result in divorce. We want to help as many couples as possible avoid that devastating progression.

The Progression of an Unhealthy Marriage

Unmet Expectations → Disillusionment → Disconnect → **Divorce**

We believe there's a much healthier progression for marriage that looks like this:

The Progression of a Healthy Marriage

Unmet Expectations ➡ Discovery ➡ Personal Responsibility ➡ **Commitment**

Sure, you may deal with some unmet expectations when you're first married. You may have imagined or expected things about your spouse that simply aren't reasonable. But as you learn to recognize the difference between healthy/reasonable expectations and unhealthy/unreasonable expectations, you enter an eye-opening phase of discovery. You learn about yourself and your mate in amazing ways. And, most important, you learn to take personal responsibility. You recognize that the only person you can truly change is yourself. As a result, you find renewed strength for your marriage and for the commitment you made to your spouse on your wedding day. You find your love growing deeper and stronger instead of dying from lack of nourishment.

We believe that God designed marriage to be a healthy, life-giving relationship. So let's begin with the "discovery" phase of what might be affecting your marriage in a negative way. Later in the book we will show you how to move your marriage toward the positive side of your expectations.

The Hopeless Romantic

When it comes to expectations in marriage, Gary and I can't help but laugh about and learn from our own experiences. I (Ted) am a hopeless, or rather, overly hopeful romantic. Without getting too cheesy, we both admit that we are the kind of guy who actually sang to our wives before our weddings. I (Gary) sang my engagement song to Norma in Palm Springs, California, in 1964. And I (Ted) sang at my own wedding. (Don't laugh.) While Randy (the judge from *American Idol*) might have described my efforts as "a bit pitchy," I remembered the lyrics word for word.

In front of my wife, Amy, and in front of our families, I belted out, "Me and You" by Kenny Chesney. I didn't just choose to sing a love song at our reception; I chose to sing a *country* love song. Even with my pitchy voice, our storybook wedding painted a few expectations in Amy's mind. To this day, we will be driving down the road and Amy will ask me to sing her that song. *Ugh!*

"Don't make me sing it, Amy, pleeeeease!" I whine.

"Come on, Ted, you know what it does to me when you sing that song."

I wish that all the expectations Amy and I carried into our marriage were as easy to meet as singing a song like "Me and You" on demand. But the truth is, there are a lot of expectations we carried into our marriage that went unspoken. And it's taken us years to learn to put them into words, say them out loud and come to terms with them in our relationship.

The truth is, I had the idea that Amy would send me off to work each day and welcome me home in parade-like fashion. And she thought I would leap through the door at night and offer long embraces with a high level of enthusiasm. I thought she would always be ready for sex. She thought our home would always be my priority above all other priorities. I thought major decisions would default to me; she assumed major decisions would be thoroughly discussed until a mutual understanding would be reached. We had a lot to learn!

As I (Gary) started to sing an engagement song I wrote for Norma, I lost my nerve and couldn't look at her for half of the song. When I looked up, she was crying and actually accepted my plea. When we announced our engagement that night at a college retreat in Palm Springs, everyone seemed surprised, because I had been dating one of the other girls in the youth group and had only broken up a few months earlier. You may have read about my typically insensitive style of manhood over the years; my engagement was reflective of how I treated Norma for the first few years of our marriage. It wasn't pretty. I allowed the engagement and announcement to be more about me rather than Norma or us.

What were some of my expectations before marriage? That we would have numerous early-morning sunrise conversations about our marriage goals, have fun all of the time, not take ourselves too seriously and live every day like a great adventure. Norma expected timeliness and orderliness in all activities, every bill paid five days before it was due, family before career and a life plan for the family.

Why were none of those expectations expressed in our wedding vows, or preferably, discussed during premarital counseling?!

The Vows

Do you remember your wedding ceremony? How about the vows you exchanged? Maybe you wrote your own vows. Ted and I both went with the traditional vows to match our very traditional weddings (Gary revised his a bit and memorized them, and then he froze up and couldn't quote them without the pastor helping him):

> *I take you _____ , to be my wife (husband), to have and to hold from this day forward, for better or for worse, for richer, for poorer, in sickness and in health, to love and to cherish; from this day forward until death do us part.*

There's a lot said in those vows, but there's also a lot that's left unsaid. What I didn't know was that those vows are loaded with Great Expectations (with a capital *G* and *E*):

What You Experienced	What You Expected
Worse	Better
Poor	Rich
Sickness	Health
End of Marriage	Marriage for a Lifetime

The result of Great Expectations is the distance between what you actually experience versus what you expected. The larger the gap between what you hoped for and what you received, the more strain you'll feel in your marriage.

The Gap and the Strain

What You Experienced . . . . What You Expected

---

Aligning Expectations with Reality

Nothing can drain the energy or life out of you like the strain caused from unrealized expectations, especially what you expect from your marriage partner. I (Gary) can remember many times when either Norma or I were upset with each other. As I reflect back on those moments, I'm amazed at how the tone of our relationship changed so quickly. Strain in a marriage can literally change a couple's attitudes toward each other like turning off a light switch. Even the littlest issues become kindling for bigger contentions. A simple decision of where to eat can become a firestorm of accusations and anger.

Let me give you an example. One morning, early in our marriage, Norma and I were driving in our camper through Prescott, Arizona. I had a craving for breakfast at a particular restaurant, and earlier in the morning, Norma had agreed to stop there; but as we drew closer to the town, she remembered another restaurant and asked, "Can we eat there instead?"

That one innocent question launched us into a three-hour battle. All kinds of issues came to the surface that had nothing to do with eggs, bacon or biscuits. Our heated discussion exposed the gap between our expectations and our experience . . . connected to something as simple as where to eat breakfast. We both expected a spectacular meal at the restaurant of our choosing, but instead we had a rather lousy meal at a restaurant neither of us liked.

As the morning pushed the limits of noon, we got back in the camper and decided to drive on to our destination. As the miles clicked by in silence, I felt exhausted. The argument with Norma wiped me out. I felt like a failure as a husband. It was as if all our progress at being a loving couple had been washed away in one three-hour torrential downpour. In the middle of this type of crisis, my personality tends to see only the negatives. We were never going to make it.

Fortunately, Norma balances me out. She sees things in a more realistic perspective. "Just look at all the things that go great between us," she gently reminded me, breaking the silence. "And this is only one speck in the scope of all the years we've been married."

That one word of encouragement gave me the energy to continue the discussion. As we talked, we realized that the issue at hand was never really about breakfast. It was about something deeper in our relationship—making sure we had healthy expectations and looking for ways to serve rather than just be served.

As for expectations, we decided that some of my unspoken expectations about our marriage—namely, *that we would always be at peace*—were just not practical or realistic. No couple can live each day without some disagreements or even major conflicts. Conflicts are inevitable and can even be healthy.

I had to develop new expectations, ones that were more pragmatic. And Norma learned that I had a huge expectation to keep the peace, and to have our children see us at peace. I hated to be in disharmony with Norma, but I expected her to follow through on her "commitments," like, "Okay, we'll eat at your favorite restaurant during a trip when I've agreed to eat there." How dare she change her mind when my mouth was already tasting those sourdough pancakes?

While driving down the highway, we both evaluated our marriage and began making a list of things we expected to receive and what we believed would be acceptable for a mutually satisfying relationship. It's amazing how just talking and agreeing on those marital basics increased our levels of energy and love for life and each other.

By the end of the discussion, I was once again energized and excited about our marriage and the rest of the trip. As for where we were going to eat lunch, well, it didn't really matter to either of us.

It's your turn to identify some of the expectations that have affected your marital satisfaction. In the next section, you will take The Great Expectations Quiz and discover what to work on to turn your disappointments into hope for a more satisfying relationship with your spouse.

Your Marital Expectations

In The Great Expectations Quiz, we have listed 78 common expectations for marriage. As you read through the list, we want you to go deeper than just saying "Yes, that's me, I have that expectation." Instead, ask yourself, "How strong is this expectation?" Remember, the greater the intensity of the expectation, the greater the gap and distance it is from healthy reality.

Rank the expectations you brought into your marriage, using a scale from 1 to 10, 1 being "not a big deal" and 10 being "I totally expected that." Rank the expectations behind your vows. For example if you planned on holding hands every day for the rest of your life, you would probably give that a 10. If holding hands was not a big deal, but you enjoyed it from time to time, you may give yourself a 5. If you didn't like holding hands, or it was not that important to you, give yourself a 1. We want you to rank the intensity, or strength, of the desire for each expectation.

The Great Expectations Quiz

On a scale of 1 to 10, place a number on the left side of the statement that represents what you expected in your marriage in this area. On the right side of the statement rank your experience of that expectation being met in your marriage (on the same scale from 1 to 10). Keep in mind that we are looking for the gaps between expectation and reality, because it is the gaps that cause the strain, disillusionment, frustration and hurt.

NOTE TO THOSE TAKING THE QUIZ

For those not yet married: Before you tie the knot, you need to get premarital counseling and/or training. As you talk through issues with a trusted pastor or leader, discuss your expectations honestly and openly. Use word pictures to describe what you long for, hope for and desire. Imagine a perfect day in marriage during your first year, your fifth year, your tenth year and your twentieth. Make sure you move beyond "We just love each other so much" to answering the deeper questions of the heart. Take "The Great Expectations Quiz" and share the score with your fiancé. Don't be afraid to be brutally honest—it will strengthen your relationship for the long haul.

For those already married: Here is a caution: You may be tempted while reading this list to respond, "Oh brother, you've got to be kidding me!" "Get over it!" or "Our puppy love went out the window a long time ago!" No matter how long ago you were married, go back to your wedding day. As you read through "The Great Expectations Quiz," what do you remember expecting on that day? What do you remember experiencing? Your marriage may be drifting—for some time—but what we are asking you to do is answer this simple question: Did I ever have this expectation at some point in my marriage relationship?

WHAT YOU HOPED FOR	EXPECTATION	WHAT YOU GOT
	1. We will have children. (If unable to have children, imagine the hurt and pain of a woman who wants to be a mom and her husband who wants to be a father.)	
	2. We will have many children.	
	3. We will have few children.	
	4. Long walks on the beach. (We will walk for no other purpose but connecting. Just me and my spouse, with the sand between our toes, our pants legs rolled up and the tide coming in.)	
	5. He will be a spiritual leader. (We will pray together, have daily devotions and attend church regularly.)	
	6. She will know how to submit.	
	7. Regular church attenders.	
	8. Nice house. (Imagine a white picket fence, furniture and backyard garden or downtown loft. Maybe not necessarily your first home, but your home a few years down the road.)	
	9. Romantic vacations. (Cruises, beach houses or remote cabins in the Rockies. The honeymoon experience will happen at least once a year.)	
	10. Regular vacations. (My spouse will take time away from the job or career each year to devote a full week to our marriage and family.)	

WHAT YOU HOPED FOR	EXPECTATION	WHAT YOU GOT
	11. Deep conversations. *(While dating, we spent hours on the phone. There will never come a day when I sense he is "rushing" me off the phone. My spouse will always love the sound of my voice.)*	
	12. Bragging on each other in public. *(While dating, we talked each other up to family and friends and showed each other's picture every chance we got. This will continue throughout our marriage.)*	
	13. Courtesy. *(Opening doors, pushing back a chair, offering a jacket on a cold night.)*	
	14. Kindness. *(We will always exchange uplifting, positive words in our communication.)*	
	15. Give up friends. *(I know that once we get married, my spouse will no longer have a desire to spend prolonged periods of time with friends. Hanging out with me will trump hanging out with friends.)*	
	16. Time with friends. *(My spouse will let me enjoy plenty of time with my friends. After all, we need relationships outside of the marriage to make life rich.)*	
	17. Great eye contact. *(When I speak, everything will stop because what I have to say will be treasured. My spouse will remove all distractions and focus on me.)*	
	18. Hand holding. *(We will hold hands at all times, in the movies, in the car, at the mall, during church and even at home.)*	
	19. Patience. *(We will never grow tired of repeating ourselves when the other person does not understand what we are saying.)*	
	20. Dress up for dates and special nights. *(My spouse will always put some thought into what he/she is wearing when we date.)*	

WHAT YOU HOPED FOR	EXPECTATION	WHAT YOU GOT
	21. *We won't change. (Our personalities and passion will not fade or change with time.)*	
	22. *Dates. (From eating out to movies, we will have a regular date night that nothing interferes with.)*	
	23. *The "I'm glad to see you" look. (When we get home from work, there will always be an overwhelming response of elation to being in each other's presence.)*	
	24. *Media will not consume our time. (Our television viewing will be limited to a show/sporting event or two a week.)*	
	25. *Freedom from addiction. (Substance abuse, alcohol, pornography will not destroy our marriage.)*	
	26. *Unconditional love. (My spouse will love me even when I am going through difficult times emotionally.)*	
	27. *Physical health. (We will remain healthy throughout our marriage. Caring for each other through major illness will not be necessary.)*	
	28. *Tenderness/gentleness. (Our words will defuse anger and encourage each other.)*	
	29. *Validation. (My spouse will always understand my fear, frustration or hurt. Listening to me will always triumph over trying to solve my problems.)*	
	30. *Together forever. (We will never leave each other. The "D" word—divorce—will never be an option for us. We are together until one of us lays the other in the arms of Jesus.)*	

WHAT YOU HOPED FOR	EXPECTATION	WHAT YOU GOT
	31. Snuggling on the couch. (Movie nights with popcorn will be a regular occurrence. Sometimes we will just snuggle with nothing to watch on TV. Just enjoying each other's presence will be enough.)	
	32. Sharing feelings. (I will always know my spouse's dreams, goals, hurts, hang-ups and frustrations. I will never have the need to guess, because there will always be a free flow of information.)	
	33. Grace and forgiveness. (The spirit of forgiveness will always exist in our home. We will not judge because we each are imperfect and make mistakes. There will be plenty of room for error.)	
	34. Devotions and prayer. (We will have a regular, daily quiet time with each other. We will work through the Bible, a book or devotional. We will pray at every meal.)	
	35. Cleanliness. (My spouse will always maintain a clean space, be it the closet, office, family room or bedroom. My spouse will always pick up and clean up his/her stuff.)	
	36. Closeness vs. close by. (We will always have a connectedness. We will never have the "in the same room, but checked out mentally" home.)	
	37. Humor/lightness. (We will never take ourselves too seriously. We know when to lighten up and when to laugh at ourselves.)	
	38. Servant, butler or maid. (We will cherish the opportunities to serve one another. We will always be that couple that refills an empty glass or picks up the dirty clothes of the other. Without hesitation or frustration we will look for opportunities to serve each other.)	

WHAT YOU HOPED FOR	EXPECTATION	WHAT YOU GOT
	39. Home-cooked meals. (My spouse will have the table set, dinner on the stove and even, at times, candles lit. Dinner out or ordered in will be infrequent. Meals will be as good as [or better than] my mom's.)	
	40. Understanding of work pressure. (We will work hard to give each other space at the end of a long day.)	
	41. Appreciation for work, job and career. (My spouse will show interest in what I do and what I contribute to the family's bottom line.)	
	42. Eyes for no other; faithfulness. (My spouse's "eyes" do not wander off of me and onto another.)	
	43. Ease of the words "I'm sorry." (Remember when you were first dating? When you would offend one another, not only did the apology come easily, but often it was repeated.)	
	44. Admission of mistakes. (My spouse will always be forthcoming with mistakes and character defects in his/her life.)	
	45. Appreciation for hobbies. (I will have no problem with the time required for my spouse's hobbies, and my spouse will have no problem with mine.)	
	46. Cared for when sick. (Did he or she prepare get-well baskets stuffed with tissue, soup, candles or a favorite magazine? That kindness will continue throughout our marriage.)	
	47. United front. (No one will ever be able to put me down to my mate. No parent, family member or friend would get away with slandering me to him/her.)	
	48. Protection. (My spouse will take a bullet for me if necessary. Sounds in the middle of the night will be quickly investigated and resolved.)	

WHAT YOU HOPED FOR	EXPECTATION	WHAT YOU GOT
	49. Companion. (We will love doing things together. We will never be one of those couples that go their separate way at movies, the mall or even at church.)	
	50. Sleeping together. (We will never sleep in separate rooms.)	
	51. Sex every day. (Regular sex will solve any lust problems.)	
	52. Creative sex. (Now I have the context to explore my sexual fantasies.)	
	53. Quickies. (She will serve me even when she is not in the mood.)	
	54. Sex all night. (We will make love until the sun comes up. Multiple orgasms will be experienced often.)	
	55. Family. (We will love each other's family and friends.)	
	56. Fondness of parents. (We will both get along well with our parents.)	
	57. Mom and Dad. (My spouse will like to hang around my mom and dad.)	
	58. Family history. (My spouse will show compassion for my family history.)	

WHAT YOU HOPED FOR	EXPECTATION	WHAT YOU GOT
	59. *Accepting my family. (We will not judge or be critical of the actions of each other's family.)*	
	60. *Time with extended family. (My spouse will love spending a lot of time with my family members.)*	
	61. *In-law visits once or twice a year. (Mom and Dad will be able to set healthy boundaries without us needing to tell them. Visits will be minimal to help us "leave and cleave.")*	
	62. *Family holidays. (My spouse will have no problem with my family taking control of the holidays.)*	
	63. *Family traditions. (My spouse will happily honor my family traditions around the holidays.)*	
	64. *Decisions. (My spouse will have no problem seeing things from my point of view.)*	
	65. *One family income. (My spouse will make plenty of money to cover our expenses so I can stay home with the kids.)*	
	66. *Financial responsibility. (My mate will hold down a good job, make a good living and provide for the needs of the home.)*	
	67. *Financial security. (We will have plenty of money to do what we need to do as a family. We will be all about paying bills on time, keeping debt to a minimum and giving to charitable organizations.)*	
	68. *Financial freedom. (My spouse will have no problem spending money freely. We will not need to keep a tight rein on the checkbook.)*	

What you Hoped For	Expectation	What you Got
	69. *Tithing. (We will give a minimum of 10 percent of our income to our church.)*	
	70. *Savings. (We will spend less than 100 percent of what we make so we have some to put into savings.)*	
	71. *Giving. (Money will be set aside to give to charitable organizations beyond our tithing.)*	
	72. *Retirement. (We will have plenty of money saved up so that we can stop working at a reasonable age.)*	
	73. *Church denomination. (We will mutually agree on the denomination for our family. My spouse will not bash my denominational preference.)*	
	74. *Theology. (We will merge our beliefs and have few theological differences.)*	
	75. *Worship style. (We will enjoy the same kind of worship experience.)*	
	76. *Entertainment. (From music to movies, we will be able to find a happy medium that both of us can enjoy.)*	
	77. *Promptness. (We will both work to be at events and family gatherings on time.)*	
	78. *Physically fit. (We will live healthy lives. Excessive weight gain will not occur.)*	

We do not want to lower your expectations. Much like raising the bar on an Olympic high jumper, we want to set goals and new challenges. When a couple has positive expectations of their marriage, their marital skills can and most likely will rise to the challenge.

After all, isn't it fair and appropriate to expect your spouse to stay faithful to you throughout your lifetime? We would never ask you to lower that expectation or remove it altogether. Yet many couples have a difficult time separating or categorizing expectations. Realistically, marital faithfulness is in a different category from the expectation of time spent with friends outside of the marriage.

We want to help you establish realistic expectations for your marriage while also challenging you to sharpen your skills as a spouse. We want to help you bridge the gap between your expectations and your actual experience in marriage.

Through the upcoming chapters, we are going to encourage you to develop and grow a healthy marital relationship. Here's a breakdown of the four overarching themes of the chapters:

The Progression of a Healthy Marriage

Unmet Expectations ➤ Discovery ➤ Personal Responsibility ➤ **Commitment**

[chapter 1]   [chapters 2–5]   [chapters 6–8]   [chapters 9–11]

We'll help you move forward by actually looking at the past and some of the deep roots that have helped you grow into who you are today. In chapter 2, you will read about four styles of parenting that have shaped your expectations and your marriage more than you realize. Then, in chapter 3, you'll take a look at the cultural influences that have subtly shaped you. Did you know that the year the generation in which you were born largely shapes the way you look at life and marriage? It's true! That's why we're going to look at how the timing of each generation's upbringing affects the way they view relationships, money and life. We'll also look at four choruses the world constantly sings to us through our culture. No matter what year you were born, you'll be able to identify these choruses in your life.

In chapter 4, we're going to delve into one of our all-time favorite topics: personality! The unique combination of personality differences in your marriage will greatly affect your expectations and the way you get along, the way you approach the future and the way you live life together. The good news is that no matter what expectations you brought into marriage because of your personality, you can learn to grow together and appreciate one another even more. We'll give you personal tips on how to get along with each personality. This information will not only help your marriage, but it will also help all of your relationships!

In chapter 5, we will take a look at how previous relationships have affected your expectations; and in chapter 6, we'll delve into one of the most crucial stages: personal responsibility. We'll show you how to re-align your expectations and take personal responsibility for the expectations you bring into your marriage.

Chapter 7 is about outrageous love. We'll give you three very specific ways you can increase the fragrance of love in your marriage and a list of more than a dozen ideas of how you can display random, loving acts toward your spouse.

Chapter 8 deals with a hot issue: *submission*. You're going to discover 10 ways to honor your spouse. But don't both spouses submit out of love for one another? Actually, husbands are asked to do something that is much harder than submission.

In chapter 9, we'll delve into *commitment*—the final stage of progress in developing healthy expectations for an exceptional marriage. You'll discover "17 Healthy Expectations You Should Have for Your Marriage."

This chapter examines what it means to take full responsibility for the commitment you made on your wedding day. Then we're going to touch on how to give your marriage a complete makeover.

Part of commitment is deciding that you're going to finish well. In chapter 10, you will learn about the four keys that will ensure your marriage stays strong to the end. You will unpack the real heart of commitment and read an unforgettable story of what it means to love until "death do us part."

Finally, we're going to look at how healthy expectations in marriage begin in one place: in you! That's why you can start building a healthy marriage even if your spouse isn't on board yet. We believe that as you read, study and discuss *As Long as We Both Shall Live,* you are going to experience a quiet but powerful revolution in your marriage and find yourself falling deeper in love with each other and with God.

FROM GARYSMALLEY.COM

Our website at GarySmalley.com receives emails each week from people asking questions about their struggling marriage. We do our best to answer these questions with biblical truth and practical insight. You will notice how many of the questions are tied to expectations for change in the other person. Whether you're a newlywed or an oldlywed, there's always more to learn when it comes to building a great relationship with your spouse. Here is a question from a woman who is disillusioned with her hoped-for fairy tale marriage.

Q: *Dating was great. Our marriage is not so great. What happened to the love and excitement we once had?*

A: Dating is all about curiosity and fascination. We spend countless hours getting to know each other. We ask great questions, diving deep into the heart of one another. The Bible tells us, in the Song of Solomon, that King Solomon paints a wonderful word picture of this stage of love:

> My dove in the clefts of the rock,
> in the hiding places on the mountainside,
> show me your face,
> let me hear your voice;
> for your voice is sweet,
> and your face is lovely (Song of Sol. 2:14).

Solomon is saying, "I want to get to know you." He loves it when she speaks and shares herself with him. He wants to communicate with her.

Marriage adds a new component to the relationship: *duty* and *responsibility*. When you were dating, you didn't share bills, household chores and childrearing. Now that you're married, you may feel like you have more duties and responsibilities than you can count!

That's why we all have to guard ourselves from becoming lousy lovers while we're being responsible spouses.

The key is to *not* replace curiosity and fascination with duty and responsibility. We must balance both sides. My wife did not fall in love with me because of my job or the fact that I was great at mowing the lawn, but because I got to know her. She felt what Solomon's bride-to-be felt a few verses later: "My lover is mine and I am his" (v. 16).

Continue to ask each other great questions to get to know each other deeply. Set a regular date night free from distractions, and keep it. Revisit some of the places you frequented on your first dates. If they are too far away, reminisce about your favorite restaurants, past vacations, your honeymoon spot, and so on.

After 40 years of marriage, I am still discovering new facets to Norma. I am very fascinated by her! I am the dreamer and she is the dream maker. She loves to investigate my dreams and figure out what I see for the future of our ministry. Then she goes to town scheduling events and travel and organizes my life by setting goals for each new dream. Her expectations for life and ministry fit perfectly with the dreams and personality God has given me. Amazing how God works all that together!

CHAPTER 2

EXPOSING DEEP ROOTS

I (Gary) grew up in a home with a mom who was truly a servant. My mom always made her children a priority and looked for ways to go the extra mile for me and my five siblings. As the youngest of six children, I was the last to leave the house, so my mom and I had a special bond.

I remember that as a teenager, I would come home from a date and my mom would be up, waiting for me. She would ask me how my evening went and then offer me a snack before heading to bed. A lot of moms might offer a glass of milk and a quick sandwich, but not my mom.

"You know what would be really great, Mom?" I'd ask.

"What, son?"

"Would you make me one of your butterscotch pies?" I'd say with a glimmer in my eyes.

Without hesitation, mom would walk into the kitchen and gather the ingredients for her scrumptious pie. I can still taste the butterscotch sweetness when I think about it now.

How spoiled was I? Do you think I was well prepared for the realities of marriage?

Without a doubt, I married an amazing woman. Norma has served me—my goals, dreams and ministry—for 44-plus years. We're like a hand in glove; I'm the dreamer and she's the dream maker. Yet somehow I sensed early in our marriage that it was not in my best interests to put in a dessert request late in the evening. Can you only imagine what Norma said to me the very first time I asked for a pie after 10:00 P.M.?

"Wake me tomorrow and tell me how it was!"

In this chapter, we want you to examine your family roots and understand how they influenced the kind of expectations you carry as an adult. We believe this discovery is essential for you to develop or retool your expectations for the health of your marriage relationship.

Self-Discovery

One of the first steps in progressing from disappointment over unmet expectations to commitment to the mate who has disappointed you is to understand what you expected from your mate and why you expected those things. The total progression looks like this:

The Progression of a Healthy Marriage

Unmet Expectations ➡ Discovery ➡ Personal Responsibility ➡ **Commitment**

For now, let's take a look at **Discovery**. You need to know where you've been and how the past has shaped you before you can recognize the ways your past affects your present. We're going to take an in-depth look at four styles of parenting that have shaped you, your personality and your marriage even more than you may realize.

Discovery: Know Your Roots

Whether you realize it or not, your parents (or those who raised you) are deeply rooted in your past and helped shape the way you live today. Parents influence and shape the way you drive a car, handle money, vote for candidates, view church and even how you approach intimacy with your spouse.

When you came into the world as an infant, you were born with a factory-installed camera. Your eyes and ears were the lens and your mind was the film or memory stick. Throughout your childhood you took pictures of the experiences around you. At home, school, church and the playground, you slowly developed these images into expectations on what life is like.

All it takes is a few hours of counseling to begin exposing some of those hidden expectations. There's nothing like sitting in front of a counselor and having him or her say, "Tell me about your childhood . . ." to stir up the memories—including the wounds and joys—of coming of age. Stories from our past can be challenging to share because they expose areas of pain and hurt. In a counseling session, all kinds of things can come to the surface, including some of the uglier things said in schoolyards and in homes. But unpacking the past is important, because your history reveals where many of the expectations you brought into marriage came from. When you understand your past, you can create a better future.

The Four Styles of Parenting

Some 30 years ago, I wrote the book *The Key to Your Child's Heart*. In it, I discussed the four parenting styles and how they affect the hearts of our children. I now see how these parenting styles contribute to the way you and I relate to our mates years later.

While many parents wish their children had come with a personal how-to manual, no child does! Instead, moms and dads everywhere are trying to figure it out—and sometimes make great and not-so-great decisions along the way. There are four primary styles of parenting. Which style did your parents use? Which style describes the way you are raising your children or want to raise your children?

The Dominant Parent

Dominant parents usually have very high standards and expectations. They are constantly raising the bar for their children and challenging them to excel. They want the very best for their kids, always keeping one

Some Typical Statements and Actions Common to the Dominant Parent:

- "Rules are rules. You're late—go to bed with no dinner."

- "I won't stand for your back talk. Apologize." (Or slap the child's face.)

- "You don't need reasons. Just do what I say."

- "I don't care how many of your friends will be there. You're not going, and I don't want to hear another word about it . . . do you hear?"

- "No son of mine is going to goof off. You took the job; you get it done."

- "How many times have I told you to stop that? Get in there—you're going to get it!"

Some Possible Reactions of Children Raised by the Dominant Parent:

- They rank lowest in self-respect. They have little ability to conform to rules or authority.

- The rigid harshness of the parent breaks the spirit of the child and results in resistance, "clamming up" or rebellion.

- The child usually does not want anything to do with his parents' rules or values. He tends to reject the ideals of his parents.

- The child may be attracted to other children who rebel against their parents and the general rules of society. They may use drugs and participate in other illegal activities.

- The child may be loud and demanding of his rights.

- In a classroom setting, the child may cause disruption in order to gain attention from others.

eye on the future. Unfortunately, the Dominant Parent seldom offers warm, caring support.

They tend to see things in black and white when it comes to their kids. They want their kids to be "raised right," but all too often Dominant Parents fail to explain the reasons for their rigid rules. They tend to be unbending and demand that their children stay away from certain activities because of their strong convictions. Because the children do not know the reasons why these activities are wrong, they may secretly participate in them.

The dominant style of parenting often results in higher aggression in younger children. This higher level of aggression usually lasts a lifetime and can lead to major violence. Harsh punishment, like washing out a child's mouth with soap, coupled with rejection, can lead to aggressive behavior.

The Neglectful Parent

Neglectful parents tend to lack both loving support and control over their children. They show an uncaring or immature attitude, lashing out at a child when pushed or irritated. These parents tend to isolate themselves from their children by excessive use of baby-sitters and to indulge in their own selfish activities. Children are viewed as a bother "to be seen and not heard."

Dr. Armand Nicholi, psychiatric professor at Harvard Medical School, helped me understand that neglectful parents are not only absent when they are physically away from home. Even when they are present they rob their children of emotional accessibility. When they are home, they usually are not listening or paying attention to their children. There are four main reasons why children are being neglected today, according to Dr. Nicholi:

1. *The high divorce rate.* Statistics show that there are more than 13 million children in single-parent homes. The divorce rate has

Some Typical Statements and Actions Common to the Neglectful Parent:

- "Work it out by yourself. Can't you see I'm busy?"

- "No! I'm expected somewhere else tonight. Get your mother to help you."

- "No, you can't stay up. Remember, you wanted to stay up late last night. Stay out of my hair!"

- "That's your problem. I've got to get to work."

- "Good grief! Can't you kids be more careful?"

- "Late again, for heaven's sake. Would someone please pass the meat?"

- "So you think I'm stupid, huh? Well, that's your problem, buddy. Just get lost!"

Some Possible Effects on Children of the Neglectful Parent:

- The harshness and neglect tend to wound the spirit of a child, resulting in rebellion.

- The child believes that he is not worth spending time with.

- The child develops insecurity because the parents are never predictable.

- The child may not develop a healthy self-respect because the child is not respected and has not learned to control himself.

- Broken promises break the spirit of the child and lower the child's self-worth.

- The child tends to do poorly in school from lack of motivation.

been spiraling upward since the early 1960s and has increased 700 percent since the beginning of the twentieth century.[1] Most divorces require single parents to work outside the home, allowing less time for the emotional development of their children. It's very difficult for single parents to provide their children with the necessary time each day for listening and emotional accessibility. However, it's not impossible.[2]

2. *The increase of mothers in the work force.* More than 55 percent of all mothers in the United States are working. This greatly increased in the 1960s, with a strong emphasis being put forth that women were unfulfilled in their homes. Economic pressures also force many women to seek jobs. By joining the work force, mothers are often less accessible to their children.[3]

3. *Excessive television viewing.* This also increased greatly in the 1960s, and now more than 99 percent of American homes have at least one television.[4] The problem with television is that even though people are physically together in a room, there is very little meaningful or emotional interaction. As parents neglect their children by watching television or other activities, the children experience an emotional loss similar to that of losing a parent through death. They often feel guilty when their parents are not with them. Some even believe the reason their parents are absent is because they are bad, and if only they were better, their parents would spend more time with them. Obviously, this awareness lowers a child's sense of worth.

4. *An increasingly mobile society.* Approximately 50 percent of Americans change their address every five years.[5] This mobility robs

Some Typical Statements and Actions Common to the Permissive Parent:

- "Well, okay. You can stay up late this time. I know how much you like this program."

- "You're tired, aren't you? A paper route is a tough job; sure, I'll take you around."

- "I hate to see you under all this pressure from school. Why not rest tomorrow? I'll say you're sick."

- "You didn't hear me call you for dinner. Well, that's all right. Sit down. I don't want you eating a cold dinner."

- "Please don't get angry with me. You're making a scene."

- "Jimmy, please try to hurry. Mommy will be late again if we don't start soon."

Some Possible Reactions of Children Raised by the Permissive Parent:

- A child senses that he is in the driver's seat and can play the parent accordingly.

- A child develops a feeling of insecurity, like leaning against a wall that appears to be firm but falls over.

- A child may have little self-respect because he has not learned to control himself and master certain personal disciplines.

- A child learns that because standards are not firm, rules can be manipulated.

children of their parents' time as well as the emotional strength and accessibility they have from friends and relatives in their former home. Yet, even if we have to move our families, we can still provide emotional accessibility to our children. We can do this by setting aside time every day to spend with each of our children or together as a family. Dr. Nicholi stressed that this time should be used to counteract the effects of our mobile society.

To illustrate how prevalent the problem of emotional accessibility is, take a short break and try spending just five minutes concentrating on your family's welfare and how you can help meet each child's emotional needs. You may find it very difficult, because we're not used to doing this in our culture.

The Permissive Parent
Permissive parents tend to be warm, supporting people, but weak in establishing and enforcing rules and limits for their children.

One of the major reasons why some parents are too permissive is because they have an inner fear that they may damage their children if they are too strict. Fear of confronting their children may actually produce the very things they fear.

On the positive side, permissive parents are strong in the area of support. I am very grateful that my parents showed me warmth and love. They were very giving, very understanding, very comforting. Effective parents realize that a certain degree of permissiveness is healthy. That means accepting that kids will be kids, a clean shirt will not stay clean for long, running will almost always be preferable to walking, a tree is for climbing and a mirror is for making faces. It means accepting that children have the right to childlike feelings and dreams. That kind of

Some Typical Statements and Actions Common to the Loving and Firm Parent:

- "You're late again for dinner, Tiger. How can we work this out together?" (Parents spend time working out solutions with the child.)

- "Hey, I wish I could let you stay up later, but we agreed on this time. Remember what you're like the next day if you miss your sleep?"

- "When we both cool off, let's talk about what needs to be done."

- "You're really stuck, aren't you? I'll help you this time. Then let's figure out how you can get it done yourself next time."

- "You say all the other girls will be there. I'd like to have more information first."

- "Did you practice your piano? I hate to do this, but we agreed—no dinner before it is finished. We'll keep the food warm for you."

- "You may answer the phone, but before you answer, you must learn to answer it the right way."

Some Typical Characteristics of Children Raised by the Loving and Firm Parent:

- The warm support and clearly defined limits tend to build self-respect within the child.

- A child is more content when he has learned to control himself.

- A child's world is more secure when he realizes there are limits that are unbending, and he understands the underlying principles why.

- Because the spirit of a child is not closed, the lines of communication are open with parents. There is less chance of the rebellious teen years.

- The children of loving and firm parents ranked highest in: (a) self-respect; (b) capacity to conform to authorities at school, church, and so on; (c) greater interest in their parents' faith in God; and (d) greater tendency not to join a rebellious group.

permissiveness gives a child confidence and an increasing capacity to express his thoughts and feelings.

Over-permissiveness, on the other hand, allows for undesirable acts, such as beating up other children, marking on buildings and breaking objects.

The Loving and Firm Parent

Loving and firm parents usually have clearly defined rules, limits and standards for living. They take time to train their children to understand these limits—like why we don't carve love notes on the neighbor's tree—and give clear warnings when a child has transgressed an established limit. But they also give support by expressing physical affection and spending personal time listening to each child. They are flexible, willing to listen to all the facts if a limit has been violated.

The loving and firm parent is a healthy and balanced combination of the dominant and permissive parent. There is firmness with clearly defined rules like, "You cannot intentionally harm our furniture or anyone else's," but this firmness is combined with loving attitudes and actions.

The Loving and Firm Parent reflects the very specific biblical instructions for parenting. It stresses two important ways that parents must take care of their children. First, they must *discipline* their children, which partly means setting clearly defined limits in the home. Second, they must follow the greatest *instruction* in Scripture—to love one another.

Knowing Your Roots

As you look at the list of parenting styles, which did you experience as a child?

___ The Dominant Parent
___ The Neglectful Parent

_____ The Permissive Parent
_____ The Loving and Firm Parent

How has that experience shaped you? How has that experience shaped your expectations of marriage and family? How have your roots affected the way you're growing into a spouse, parent and follower of Christ?

Gary and I both realize that our roots have shaped us. The way we were raised was very different from each other, but our family roots have played a significant role in our approach to marriage and life.

Gary's Roots: The Permissive Parent

My mother and father were very warm and loving and accepting of me. But my father was more distant, and as far as I can remember, there were no rigid rules in our home. My parents usually gave in to my demands. Even when I was in trouble, they would not spank or discipline me. My mother said she never spanked because her first child died of blood poisoning and she had spanked her two weeks before she died. She made my father promise to never spank any one of their five remaining children.

Although they meant well, that leniency affected me negatively. My parents left all decisions concerning how I would spend my spare time up to me. In fact, I didn't start formally dating until . . . the third grade! This caused a number of problems in my life.

Once my father caught me in a serious infraction as a young boy. From his firm voice I knew that I was in trouble. Later he said he would let me off without punishing me if I promised not to do it again. I actually told him that I needed a spanking, but he wouldn't do it. There was something in me that wanted to be corrected.

I found the same permissiveness in school. Once a teacher caught me passing notes in the third grade after warning me of the consequences if

I didn't stop. She sent me to the principal. He talked to me for a while, told me I needed to shape up, then said that he was going to spank me. I thought he really meant business, but about 15 minutes later, he said he was going to give me another chance if I promised not to pass notes again. Of course, I promised the world, but inwardly I can remember being disappointed that he didn't follow through.

Last summer, while we were vacationing with our daughter and her family, Norma announced that she grew up in a Quaker home. I had never before heard my bride refer to her upbringing as Quaker. The entire family peppered her with questions, wanting to know what this meant. What's funny is that my 11-year-old granddaughter loves Norma so much that she now wants to be a Quaker, even though she has no idea what it means.

Norma remembers that the Quaker's "biggies" were rules—what she could and couldn't do. She was not allowed to drink, dance or miss church. And the three of those were just the beginning. Norma grew up with a rule for everything, a far cry from how I was raised. Norma had structure; I had none. Her parents watched and guarded her every move. My parents did not even know where I was until I came home to sleep

While it can be a great deal of fun to discover the differences in how each person has been raised, it can also be a subliminal source of stress and frustration. We see that clearly at times in our work together at the Smalley Relationship Center. Norma runs the operations of our company; I provide the content. When you think about it, it really is a simple setup. However, that is not always the case.

Our staff meetings are a prime example. I lead a meeting with no structure. Norma steps into meetings with budgets and calendars. With me, there is no telling where the meeting may end up. With Norma, we have an agenda and a clear plan of where we are going. And here is where her past and mine collide.

When I step into an executive team meeting and announce that we are restructuring the company, Norma is at a loss. She is at a loss because rules, structure and organization run through her veins. When I declare that we are starting another nonprofit company for the purpose of helping marriage and families, Norma is thinking about IRS forms, accountants, attorneys, recent changes in legislation and how this will affect the staff and organization. There is a definite and right way of doing things, and my permissive background sets no boundaries. Many times I feel as though all of the details will just take care of themselves. Norma, with her background, knows differently. So how do we merge these two diverse backgrounds?

The answer is simple, and we plan on showing you how to do it throughout this book. Norma and I have thrived in marriage these many years because of one simple fact: We both understand each other's personality and background. What's very important is that we both respect each other's backgrounds and see the value in each other! And we have both committed our lives to helping marriages and families. How we operate on a day-to-day basis may be completely different, but we have the same mission to complete.

Ted's Roots: The Dominant Parent

I grew up in a dominant home. To be fair, because my parents are still living and I love them very much, I need to explain that we were involved in a church that taught this model of parenting.

So I grew up in an independent, fundamental, premillennial, only *King James Bible* Baptist church. And I had issues. I was dragged to church Sunday morning, Sunday night and Wednesday night (and any other night of the week my pastor desired). This dominant style of parenting only fed my guilt-prone nature.

A while back, Amy and I took the kids to Disneyland. Because of the way I was raised, pedestrian signs are equivalent to law. You follow the signs and you obey them no matter what. For my wife, signs are just suggestions for other people. So we were enjoying the day at Disneyland and had a huge double stroller for when the kids were tired of walking. You would think there should be an engine in this stroller it was so big!

In the early afternoon, our son, Carson, fell asleep in the stroller. I'm pushing him around when Amy decides she wants to take our daughter, Corynn, into a kids' crafts area. That's when I see the sign: "No Strollers Beyond This Point."

"Come on!" Amy said.

"Do you really think that sign is for everybody but you?" I protest.

"Ted, they understand if the baby falls asleep in the stroller and that you can't leave your baby out in the stroller when you go on a ride or do an activity," she argues. "Of course, you can come in."

"It says that nowhere on the sign," I said. "If they would explain that on the sign, I would listen to it. I'm staying out here with the stroller."

The crafts area was vacant. Amy and Corynn were the only ones working on a project. As I pushed Carson back and forth in the stroller outside the marked line, I watched Amy pop her head up and mouth several words to me. (We're so good at communication in our marriage that we don't even need to use audible tones anymore.) I knew what she was saying. She motioned me to come in. I could feel the peer pressure mounting—and it's from my own wife!

Finally, I gave in. That's right, as a full-fledged pastor, I looked both ways and snuck a stroller into a forbidden area in Disneyland. That's not one of my best moments, but I wanted to keep my wife happy. Well, I'm not inside 30 seconds when a dwarf from Cinderella's entourage walked up to me and said, "Sir, didn't you see the sign?"

I glance over at my wife, who I love with all my soul, and realize that at this moment she has completely disowned me! She wouldn't make eye contact with me or the dwarf.

"Yes, I saw the sign," I said, looking down at the stroller.

"Sir, I'm going to need you to go up to that area," he said, pointing outside.

After completing the craft with Corynn, Amy walked out, took one look at my disgruntled face and said, "Oh, you big baby."

"You big baby!" I exclaimed. "We broke a rule! The rule said no strollers. And by the way, we signed a covenant agreement. We are bonded for life, and you disowned me down there!"

"You're so dramatic!" she said.

The worst part was that she was right. My wife lives with a sense of reckless abandon that is so refreshing to me. Meanwhile, I was walking through Disneyland like a paranoid freak, afraid that Cinderella and her gang were going to arrest me for breaking the baby stroller rule. As we walked through the park, I realized that my guilt-prone nature and rules-oriented background were rearing their ugly head. Later that afternoon, Amy gently reminded me, "Ted, never forget that Jesus has set you free. You don't need to live in bondage to the past." And I needed to hear that.

Looking back, I realized that my guilt-prone nature was the source for so much of the confusion and frustration in the early years of our marriage. Amy and I went straight from our wedding to a small Southern Baptist Church in South Georgia where I served as an associate pastor for two years. I still have great affection for the great folks that make up Southside Baptist Church in Lakeland, Georgia. My role there was to lead the youth and worship, and the responsibilities kept me at the church several nights a week. In other words, every time the doors were open, we were there.

After Southside, we moved to Dallas so I could attend Dallas Theological Seminary. I'll never forget the weirdness of our first week there. I had taken a job 45 hours a week in the IT department of a civil engineering firm, plus I was taking 12 credit hours at seminary. Life was packed. Amy worked as a school teacher. We were also in the hunt for a great church to plug into. During our first week something happened that to this day Amy will not let me forget.

It was Wednesday afternoon when I called Amy and asked if she would be open to checking out The Heights, a large Baptist church on Highway 75 north out of Dallas. She agreed to check it out.

Keep in mind, this is Wednesday and every good and proper child of God goes to church on Wednesday night (I say that in love and humor toward all our readers). As we pulled into the parking lot, there were only a dozen cars or so. The parking lot was built for thousands. But this did not alarm me because I knew a smaller percentage of the Sunday crowd attended during the week.

We walked in the front doors and were greeted by a very gracious staff member: "Good evening. How can I help you?"

"We're here for church," I blurted out.

The staff member, who was actually heading out the door for the day, said "We actually do not have a service tonight."

"What programs are you offering?" I asked.

The staff member looked quite puzzled and did not know what to say. After scrambling through a bulletin left over from Sunday, he finally was able to point to one class meeting upstairs in the fellowship hall that night.

"We'll take it," I said as though I was buying scalped tickets for the last two seats at the World Series.

Within minutes we had Bibles open alongside 15 or so members of a senior adult Bible study led by the senior adult pastor of the church. I listened intently and took notes. Halfway through I looked over at Amy and she rolled her eyes at me. Those rolled eyes can be interpreted: "What the heck are we doing here?"

Afterward, we headed to the Pasta House for dinner and a little light conversation.

"Ted, what was that all about?" Amy asked.

"What do you mean?" I asked back. I love answering a question with a question.

"Don't get me wrong, they were very sweet people, but did we just join a senior adult Bible study?" she asked. Still no answer.

"No, but we will need to keep looking for a church," I said.

She patiently went deeper: "Ted, you are taking three theological classes this semester and working 45 hours a week. Do we need more activity and Bible studies?"

Then it hit me! Twenty-two years of a dominant environment just fell away. She did not have to say another word. I got it. We spent the next two hours in one of the best "expectations" conversations we had ever had. To this day, we still laugh about that night.

When you come to terms with your roots, you can grow into all that God has for you, your marriage and your future. You can learn why you respond to certain situations in a certain way as well as learn the roots of your spouse's responses. And as you discover the way each other ticks—and why you tick that way—then you have grace to grow closer together and learn to love each other more deeply.

Recognizing your roots is only the first step in gaining a healthy perspective on the expectations you've carried into your marriage.

The next factor we need to look at is how culture is affecting your expectations. In chapter 3, we're going to look at the cultural influences that are quietly (and loudly) shaping you. We're going to help you identify which of four generations you belong to and how this shades the way you approach marriage and relationships. Then, we're going to look at the four choruses that culture tries to get us to sing along with. Just recognizing them will help you and your spouse stay on tune with who God has created you to be!

FROM GARYSMALLEY.COM

This question was sent to our website by a woman who has trouble forgiving her parents for what they put her through as a child.

Q: *My dad and mom are no longer living, and I still have a hard time forgiving them for divorcing when I was 11. I have held it in for my entire life and feel as though much of the grief in my own life is a direct result of the poor example set by my folks. How can I forgive dead parents and move on with my life?*

A: Your question is a great start to recovery. The truths you embrace about forgiveness will help all of your relationships, but especially the way you relate to your spouse, especially if his behavior reminds you of the parenting style of one of your parents.

Paul said in Romans 12: "Do not repay anyone evil for evil. Be careful to do what is right in the eyes of everybody. If it is possible, as far as it depends on you, live at peace with everyone" (vv. 17-18). Basically what Paul is saying is that while it is no longer possible for you to be face to face with your mom and dad, you can still forgive them. Not for their sake, but for yours. You need to rid your body of the poison you have been drinking called bitterness and resentment. The verse says, "As far as it depends on you." The issue of forgiveness is at the core of personal responsibility. Your anger and unforgiveness toward your mom and dad have held you back. Your victim's approach to life has thwarted God's best for you.

You cannot reverse the parenting you had. That is not possible. You cannot relive your childhood and redirect your mom and dad. In other words, you have zero responsibility for the way you were raised. Not one person on the planet had a choice in their parents. But there is something we do get to choose. We get 100 percent responsibility for the choice of where we go today.

Release the hurt. Release the past. Once you turn this over to the Lord, you will then be able to *live at peace with everyone*. You will no longer be held hostage or powerless in life. You will change once you begin to resolve your anger.

Your best days are ahead of you. Learn from this and help others to keep from drinking that poison of unresolved anger.

You cannot take responsibility for what happened to you with your parents in the past, but moving forward is your responsibility. You have a choice to make. You can choose to live the rest of your days as a victim of your past. Or you can choose to embrace personal responsibility and be an example for generations to come.

CHAPTER 3

CULTURAL INFLUENCES

If you have ever met a Baby Buster, that person grew up with the same kind of cultural influences that I did. If you have ever met a Boomer, you've met someone that's a lot like my dad.

Two years after we were married, Amy and I left a great church and job in South Georgia and headed to Dallas for my seminary training. In addition to my 45-hour workweek as a network administrator, and three classes at the seminary, I took a part-time position as a worship leader on weekends at First Baptist Church in Little Elm, Texas. We were time crunched to say the least.

The civil engineering firm I worked for was a hard-charging group of Boomers. The official schedule for work was 7:30 A.M.–5:30 P.M. Since my classes started at 6:30 P.M., I had to hightail it out of there to fight traffic and make it to class. The only problem and pressure I faced, though, was standing alone at the elevators every night at 5:30 P.M. Nobody else was leaving. I would get these weird stares from my colleagues. Some would even walk by and under their breath say, "Must be nice," or "Hey there, part-time."

Then there was my marriage. I had way too much going on and I knew it was causing struggles at home. I had to do something about that. Decisions needed to be made in order for us to survive, let alone thrive!

It was a Friday afternoon just a month into the new job when I hit bottom. I knew only one person to call for help and encouragement: my dad. With tears in my eyes, I dialed the phone in my six-by-six-foot cubicle.

"Hey, Dad," I spoke softly.

"Hey, son," he responded.

"I'm not doing too good, Dad."

"What's going on?" he asked.

I unloaded, or maybe I should say, I downloaded: "This just is not working. Amy and I are stressed with moving to a new city, starting seminary and getting settled. Dad, you worked more than 30 years in corporate life; how did you do it? The pressure here to work ridiculous hours is overwhelming. I'm not lazy. I have two jobs, three if you count seminary. I'm concerned that this will all be too much for Amy to handle. What should I do?"

"Well, Ted, you sure had it good back there in Georgia," he said.

I was disappointed and frustrated by my dad's response. He was reminding me that we should have stayed in Georgia where people loved us, where we had a balanced life and worked reasonable hours. I wanted him to support me emotionally where I was, not where I had been. To my dad, what I was describing seemed like normal life pressures. But to me, it was a very big deal.

What I didn't realize is that my struggle with expectations regarding my life, marriage and work were linked to something bigger than myself. They were a direct result of the culture and generation in which I was raised. Meanwhile, my dad's counsel came directly from the generation and culture in which he was raised.

In this chapter, we're going to look at some differences between four generations and how the generation in which you grew up shapes your expectations of marriage. Then we will examine cultural influences, including movies, songs and television shows that try to get us to settle for less than God's best in our life, our relationships and our marriage.

The Four Generations

Not enough people talk about the important link between marital conflict and the generation in which a person is born. Let's look at four distinct generations to better understand how the time period in which you were born affects your attitudes, reactions and expectations regarding your marriage and other relationships. In addition, you'll get a glimpse into other generations. Pay special attention to the generation that grew up before yours and after yours; you will discover what those generations are prone to struggle with. Discovery (knowledge) is power! In this case, power to understand your spouse and other family members. The purpose in looking at the different generations is to help you discern the messages written on your heart through culture and how they shape your marital expectations. That is the first step to bridging the gap between your expectations and real life.

Keep in mind that you may have some characteristics from another generation too. For instance, I (Gary) am a Builder, but I take on many of the characteristics of a Boomer. Ted is a Buster, but after hanging around him for many years, I have noticed Boomer tendencies in him. Maybe that is why we get along so well!

Generation No. 1: Builders

If you were born between 1922 and 1943, you are a Builder. Some of the defining events in your life include the Great Depression and World War II. You tend to value hard work; law and order (not just the TV show); and respect for authority. This generation remembers when dinner was earned day to day—six or seven days a week—and most people grew up turning on the radio for entertainment.

The Builder generation is also called the "Greatest Generation." I want to give you some big-picture words—ideas—about this generation. This is the generation of sacrifice. This is the generation that not only saved the world for us, but built this country for us. They built it through sacrifice and hard work. They were willing to sweat to death to get the job accomplished. They are people of duty, loyalty and honor.

Once these people took a job, they didn't quit it. Once they took a job, they stuck with it and went through more bosses than anybody due to their longevity at work.

BUILDER EXPECTATIONS

STAY MARRIED

WORK THROUGH ISSUES

WORK HARD

TO THE KIDS: "I DIDN'T HAVE IT,

SO YOU DON'T NEED IT."

I think about the couple that had been married for 75 years. They stood before the judge and said, "We're getting a divorce." The judge said he had to ask why they would get divorced now after 75 years of marriage. The old guy looked at his wife and then the judge and said, "Well, we decided to wait until the kids died."

That is the Builder generation. They have great loyalty, a hard work ethic and are willing to sacrifice. Here's another trait: thriftiness.

We do not see a lot of Builders at our marriage seminars. Not because they cannot afford them, but because they do not think they need them. Builders often tell us, "Ater 50 years of marriage, what else is there? What could we possibly learn to make our marriage better?" This "hard work" generation can develop an "If it ain't broke, don't fix it" attitude when it comes to marriage. Enrichment is not a big deal to builders. Why? They grew up in survival mode. That is why they work so hard. But when that attitude creeps into marriage, it can become a vacuum devoid of intimacy.

Generation No. 2: Baby Boomers

The Baby Boomers are those born between 1943 and 1960. Some of the defining events of their lives include the invention of the television, the civil rights movement and the prosperity that America experienced after World War II. A boomer tends to value health and wellness, personal growth and involvement in the culture.

The first half of this generation grew up watching the Lennon Sisters sing their harmonies on *The Andy Williams Show*. They sat with great anticipation in their living rooms as Neil Armstrong walked on the moon in 1969. They grew up talking publicly about sex in a way their parents never talked about it.

The Baby Boomers tend to live to work rather than work to live. They tend to be very efficient and look for ways to get things done quickly and effectively. They find success in accomplishment and acquired wealth.

BOOMER EXPECTATIONS

LONGEVITY IN MARRIAGE

MASK MARITAL STRUGGLES TO FRIENDS AND FAMILY

WORK LONG AND BE SUCCESSFUL

TO THE KIDS: "I DIDN'T HAVE IT, BUT I'M

GOING TO MAKE SURE YOU GET IT."

If Boomers are having marital problems, you rarely know about it. They can fight and argue the whole way to church, but when the car hits the parking lot, it's nothing but smiles. They will even hold hands while walking into the building. That is why small groups are so challenging for many in the Boomer generation. They do not feel that other people need to know about their "dirty laundry." Another favorite saying of Boomers would be, "Our marriage is fine." You don't know that Boomers are having marital struggles until the relationship is at the point of crisis. Then they will get help. Unlike their builder parents, Boomers are able to get to the point where they admit something is broken in their marriage and go for help. Builders will just accept such a problem as "normal."

Generation No. 3: Busters

The Buster generation includes those born between 1960 to 1980. Some of the defining events for this generation are Watergate, the fall of the Berlin Wall and the influence of MTV. Busters tend to value diversity, global thinking and pragmatism.

If you are a Buster, there's a good chance you rolled up your pant legs as part of a regrettable fashion trend, played Trivial Pursuit and watched Michael J. Fox in all three *Back to the Future* movies.

Because Boomers were working so efficiently, many Busters grew up without a real connection to their parents or family. Many never heard the words "I love you" from one or both parents. Instead, love was expressed through material provision or gifts. Many Busters were latchkey kids, and as a result, they struggle with what a healthy marriage looks like.

Busters tend to work to live and have fun on the weekends. They know that if one job doesn't work out, they can find another. Busters tend to have more jobs by the age of 30 than their parents ever dreamed of in a lifetime. Busters also struggle with a sense of entitlement and wanting everything their parents had, after working 20-plus years, right after graduation (high school or college).

BUSTER EXPECTATIONS

GIVE MARRIAGE A SHOT

DIVORCE IS AN OPTION

WORK AS MUCH AS NECESSARY

BE GREAT PARENTS AND OKAY LOVERS

TO THE KIDS: "I DIDN'T HAVE IT, BUT

YOU'LL GET EVERYTHING."

My (Ted's) generation struggles with entitlement. This state of mind is bringing a kind of stress to our generation that no other generation has experienced before. It has created crisis in our marriages because we are buying cars and homes we cannot afford and changing jobs as often as the wind blows. The overextension of our finances coupled with a lack of stability in our work ethic has created great uncertainty for the future.

This sense of entitlement can also lead us to switch spouses as frequently as we switch jobs. My friend Larry had five jobs last year. When we met for lunch one day he told me that the job market was not working out for him. When I probed deeper, I discovered something about Larry that is not only true of the Buster work ethic but also true of their marital ethic.

"Why so many jobs?" I asked.

"Ted, you wouldn't believe this, but I had five bad jobs because I had five bad bosses," he said.

"Five bad bosses . . . I can't believe it. What are the chances?" I said, "How's your sixth job and boss working out?"

"This one ain't looking much better," he said.

That is when I knew I had to share with Larry *The Common Denominator* principle.

"Larry, I need to share something very profound with you: Wherever you go, there you are."

He looked puzzled, so I continued to explain by saying, "Larry, there has been one constant to every job you have had. Do you know what that is? Can you figure out the common denominator?"

"What?" he asked.

"You!"

"Every boss was unrelenting if I showed up a little late," he said. "Every boss expected me to work five days a week. Come on, Ted, what's wrong with a guy wanting to take a little time off?"

"Larry, you have got to figure this out," I said. "If you aren't careful, this same attitude will follow you into marriage one day. I know you are not married to your job, but you plan on marrying one day, don't you?"

"You bet," he said.

"Then you must begin working on taking personal responsibility for your life. Your boss and your soon-to-be wife are not the sources of all your problems and shortcomings. Becoming an adult has nothing to do with your age, but it has everything to do with when you make the decision to own 100 percent of your thoughts, emotions, words and actions. That means that you never again blame others for what you are doing."

Larry is no different from most Busters I meet and counsel with. The Builder and Boomer generations were forced to grow up at an early age. Many were forced to go to work at an early age for their survival. Because the Busters were handed everything and had to work for very little, they often do not understand work (in the marketplace or in the home) until later in life. Many Busters I work with are not becoming adults until their thirties or even their forties.

Generation No. 4: Bridgers

Bridgers are those born after 1980. They are also called "millennials" or "mosaics." Some of the defining events and trends for this generation include school violence, multiculturalism and the popularity of reality TV. Bridgers tend to value civic duty, achievement and diversity.

X-box, iPods and anything technical define this generation. The Bridgers are teaching the Busters, Boomers and Builders how to use technology. Information, good and bad, is available to them in a way it never was to previous generations. For example, Busters and Boomers bought albums and CDs, many of which were filled with songs they never listened to, but they paid full price anyway. The Bridgers pay 99 cents a song on iTunes and buy only the ones they want to listen to.

This iPod generation is still in the process of defining themselves. Bridgers want to live, not live to work. They desire fully defined expectations at work. When they fulfill those expectations, they want to go home—preferably before 5:00 P.M. based on a flexible work hours option. Once home, they want to spend time with their family—particularly with their kids. They want to love on their children by spending time together.

BRIDGER EXPECTATIONS
DELAY MARRIAGE
WAIT FOR COMPATIBILITY IN SOUL MATE
WORK SMARTER, NOT HARDER
INFORMATION AT THE TOUCH OF A BUTTON

The Bridger Generation will be the fastest generation so far to walk the face of the earth.

As much as technological advances have improved our quality of life, it has its downside. Frankly, I (Ted) am scared to death for the Bridger marriage. The rate of sexual addiction among young adults is staggering. It is the secret sin we don't like to talk about. Yet it is single-handedly corrupting our society—destroying marriages, families, careers and even churches.

When Gary and I were growing up, access to sexually explicit material wasn't that easy. Movies and magazines were exchanged discreetly in basements or fields. A startling survey recently revealed that 50 percent of Christian men and 20 percent of Christian women admit that they are addicted to pornography. Not just struggling . . . addicted. That's 84 million Christians.[1]

The Culture Factor

Every generation "owns" a signature music style, and modern generations also have another powerful component that expresses their generation:

movies! Gary and I are huge movie buffs. (Honestly, I don't know what we love more: the movies or the popcorn.)

It may be subtle, but movies and music have the power to shape what we expect out of our marriages. If we turn off our filters (those little switches in our brain that allow emotion to override reason), we can end up allowing messages to seep into our hearts that don't belong there.

I (Gary) am a hopeless romantic. One of my all-time favorite movies is *Pride and Prejudice*. Brought back to the big screen in 2005, this Jane Austen classic teaches us the power of love and commitment.

When the beautiful Elizabeth Bennett meets handsome Mr. Darcy, she swears that she will never marry such a man. If he were the last man on earth, she would stay single until death. But adventure takes over. Through a series of events, she finds herself in love with the man she once could not stand. I love the movie for many reasons. Witty dialogue, adventure and romance are the perfect ingredients in a great love story.

I sometimes believe that Norma and I live in a giant novel, with a new chapter being written each day. One reason the Jane Austen movie had such a profound impact on me was because it is my marriage unfolding on the screen. Norma and I could not be more different from each other. When Norma first met me, she said, "No way!" She was looking for someone entirely different from me. But through the years, the adventures we have experienced together, the laughter and the romance have bonded us as a couple.

I (Ted) prefer action and adventure flicks. My favorite films are the ones that depict the threat of world extinction. You might think—*yuck, how morbid!* But these movies have actually had a significant impact on the way I treat my family—in a good way.

One of my favorite movies of all time is *Deep Impact*. Morgan Freeman plays the president of the United States. He announces to the whole world that a meteor is heading to earth. Throughout the whole movie, you know exactly how much time is left before the meteor impacts earth.

With the announcement that there are only 30 days left, we get glimpses into different people's lives and how they choose to spend their time. One character, who had been estranged from her father for years, decides to say the words to her dad she should have said years before. The portrait of reconciliation in their relationship is beautiful.

That one movie, combined with Tim McGraw's song "Live Like You Were Dying," has caused me to love more deeply, speak more sweetly, and forgive my family and friends more quickly.

What would you do if you had only 30 days left to live? How would you adjust your priorities? Movies and music are so effective in helping us answer those questions because they touch our emotions. When something touches your emotions, you remember it for a lifetime. That's why you remember lyrics to songs more easily than entries you've read in the encyclopedia. Movies and music have the power to do just that!

Last night, we were coming home from dinner when a huge deer jumped in front of the vehicle. We were traveling about 50 mph, hit the deer and crunched the front drivers side of the car. Somehow, in that split second, I was able to keep my hands on the wheel and respond well.

Keep your hands on the steering wheel. Don't make any sudden moves. When I was finally able to pull over to inspect the damage, I couldn't open the driver's door. I had to exit Amy's passenger door. While we were walking around the vehicle, we didn't realize that our four-year-old, Corynn, had managed to unbuckle her seatbelt and get out of the vehicle. She came running toward me, screaming, "There's fur! There's fur!"

When I looked around, I realized the deer had retreated to the forest and there was nothing we could do.

After comforting our daughter, Amy and I got back in the car. She said, "I knew this day was coming. With your driving, this day was going to happen, but I'm really surprised at how well that went. You really handled that well."

I smiled. I guess watching NASCAR had paid off!

The vehicle was able to start and, fortunately, we were only a mile from home. For the remaining drive home, we were praising our Father in heaven for His protection.

The whole incident was a reminder to make every day count and make every relationship right. Reconciliation should be the order of every day. Think about it for a moment. What would you do if you only had 30 days left to live? From whom would you need to ask forgiveness? To whom do you need to offer forgiveness? What have you left unsaid that needs to be spoken aloud?

Movies like *Deep Impact, Armageddon* and *The Day After Tomorrow* are all movies that tackle this subject. These stories remind me of James 4:13-14: "Now listen, you who say, 'Today or tomorrow we will go to this or that city, spend a year there, carry on business and make money.' Why, you do not even know what will happen tomorrow. What is your life? You are a mist that appears for a little while and then vanishes."

I can't tell you the number of times I've watched a movie and had a Bible verse come to mind. A scene will remind me of a verse and compel me to reflect on Scripture. But then there are those times when a verse flashes through my mind for the exact opposite reason.

Mixed Messages

Messages have seeped into our hearts through the media of music and movies. It's important to identify and clarify those messages to see how they have translated into expectations for your marriage and spouse. What you choose for entertainment may be influencing you more than you realize! You make thousands of decisions a day based on your worldview. As we learned from chapter 2, much of your worldview—the lens through which you view life—came from your parents. But once you left your parents' home, your worldview was and is still being shaped by what you expose yourself to.

Four Choruses That Will Undermine Your Marriage

Whether you realize it or not, you may be feeding your mind and emotions unhealthy thoughts and beliefs through media. Now, that doesn't mean you need to unplug your iPod or TiVo for the rest of your life. But it does mean that you need to take time to regularly evaluate what you believe, why you believe it and what is influencing your belief system. You need to know the song that is playing in your head! Does it breathe life and hope and joy in you? Or is the chorus in your mind one that contributes to unhealthy expectations, selfishness and fear? Here are a few choruses you've probably heard sung and scripted in the shows and songs you enjoy. They may seem innocent, but don't be deceived. They can undermine your marriage and the plans God has for your life.

Chorus No. 1: It's Mine, All Mine

You've probably heard this chorus sung through shows like *The Apprentice*, *Survivor* and *Who Wants to Be a Millionaire?* The chorus "It's Mine, All Mine" echoes both loud and clear, and quietly and subtly. This chorus has another name: materialism. Materialism can be defined as simply wanting more. When combined with the expectation that "more" is deserved, the result is entitlement. Have you ever been around people who feel entitled all the time? They're not much fun to be around. They're the kind of people who will help themselves to anything in your kitchen when you haven't offered. They'll borrow things without asking. They'll be gravely disappointed with you whenever you don't say yes to their latest need, request, or whim.

How do you know if this chorus is influencing your life? You can recognize its presence whenever your valuables determine your value. You can get to the bottom of your heart's priorities by asking yourself: What is the order of my spending on payday? Do I pay bills, get a few extras, then save and give? Or is giving and saving a priority?

Don't try keeping up with the Joneses, because the Joneses are in debt.

Jesus reminded His disciples, "A man's life does not consist in the abundance of his possessions" (Luke 12:15). And Solomon wisely said, "The abundance of a rich man permits him no sleep" (Eccles. 5:12). In other words, the more you have, the more you have to take care of. A bigger house means more cleaning. A bigger car means more gas at the pump. A bigger job title means more hours and responsibility. Bigger is not always better.

I constantly have to guard myself against this chorus. I recently found a door-buster early-bird sale for a 52-inch high definition television for only $474. All we had to do was get up at 3:00 A.M.! I told Amy about the promotion, and she said, "It's unbelievable! But we already have several TVs."

She was right. And I needed her voice to help me stop humming along with the chorus of materialism.

Chorus No. 2: Me, Myself and I

You may recognize this chorus because it's one of the most popular! We see it displayed in the life of everyone from movie stars and famous musicians to the neighbor next door. The chorus is simply: It's all about me. If you've ever seen the TV "soap-drama" *Desperate Housewives,* you've seen this chorus sung loud and clear!

This self-centered chorus goes beyond natural concern for one's health, welfare and future and turns into an obsession. The "Me, Myself and I" chorus never sings about the kids, the spouse or the other employees at the company. The lyrics remind us that status, success and salary define who you are and give you worth. Because significance is found in possessions, it's usually not too long until your possessions possess you! With a naval-gazing, me-centric focus, it's impossible to know what it means to be in a loving relationship with God, let alone with others. The result is the hollow satisfaction that comes with acquiring temporal things.

Jesus said that if you try to keep your life for yourself, you will lose it (see Luke 17:33). Only by losing your life—giving it up to God—can you find abundant life.

Chorus No. 3: If It Feels Good, Do It

Mick Jagger expresses this chorus best in the song "I Can't Get No Satisfaction." My only problem with the song is that Jagger still wears leather pants. Don't you think it's time we put an age limit on rockers who want to wear leather pants?!

When I listen to Jagger's song, I can't help but wonder, *Why can't he get any satisfaction?*

Someone singing the "If It Feels Good, Do It" chorus is a pleasure seeker, loves the thrill of the moment and pursues whatever feels good. Comfort becomes the ultimate good.

Is pleasure bad? No, but it's a by-product of living right, not the purpose of life. People who pursue pleasure above all else are called hedonists. Hedonists never get enough excitement or thrill. Just as soon as they finish one pleasurable experience they're ready for the next.

Galatians 5:13 reminds us, "It is absolutely clear that God has called you to a free life. Just make sure that you don't use this freedom as an excuse to do whatever you want to do and destroy your freedom" (*THE MESSAGE*).

One of my favorite candy bars in the whole world is Snickers. Years ago, they had an advertising campaign based on the idea, "Snickers satisfies you." It's a great tag line except for one little problem: When I finish eating one Snickers bar, I immediately want another. This is particularly true when it comes to the fun-sized mini-Snickers. I can literally eat those all day long. Which makes me wonder, *Does Snickers really satisfy?* My waistline tells me Snickers makes me want more.

This chorus "If It Feels Good, Do It" will leave you wanting more. It is the law of diminishing returns. The more pleasure we crave and seek to satisfy our hurts and pains, the less it will do for us. God never intended for pleasure to fill the gaping hole in our souls.

Chorus No. 4: To Each His Own

"To Each His Own" might sound like a catchy chorus, but it's one that you don't want to get caught by. If you sing this enough times, you'll find your worldview blurred by two myths.

The first one is called the *Situational Myth*. The situational myth suggests that whatever situation you find yourself in, all you need to do is adapt truth to make that work. People singing this part of the chorus believe they can't tell others how to make a decision or live their life. After all, what works for you may not work for me. The result is relativism. You end up basing your ethics on whatever is happening at the time.

The second is the *Sincerity Myth*. It doesn't matter what you believe or how you live it out so long as you are sincere. The problem with this myth is that you can be sincerely wrong.

When these two myths blend, you find yourself singing "To Each His Own." As long as the consequences don't catch up with your actions, you feel like everything is fine. The problem is that, more often than not, everything is not fine, and someone needs to speak up and stand up for what's right in a loving way.

"To Each His Own" will prevent you from confronting others in a biblical manner and also being confronted by those who love you most. This chorus will prevent you from growing into all that God has called and created you to be. In a marriage, it can be devastating.

Three Keys to Balancing the Culture and the Truth

So which chorus have you been singing or been tempted to sing? Maybe you've combined a couple of those choruses. If so, the principles that follow will help you begin to sing a different tune—one that will guide you to life-giving truth and fulfillment God's way.

Filter the World Through the Word

Romans 12:2 advises, "Do not conform any longer to the pattern of this world, but be transformed by the renewing of your mind. Then you will be able to test and approve what God's will is—his good, pleasing and perfect will." Meanwhile, Proverbs 15:14 tells us, "A wise person is hungry for truth, while the fool feeds on trash" (*NLT*).

On the stage of truth stand *experience, emotion, reason, tradition* and *Scripture*. Downstage, in prime position, is God's Word. What you experience in life is not necessarily wrong but needs to be viewed through the truth of what the Bible says. Your emotions are not a right or wrong issue, but your feelings toward life and your marriage need to be filtered by God's truth.

Some would put the traditions of the church on the same level as Scripture. But what the church fathers say about truth is not on the same level as the Bible. We do the same thing with our opinions of truth; we like to elevate our opinions to the same level as absolutes. Opinions can be on the stage with truth, so long as they are filtered through Scripture. And finally, our ability to reason with truth is great, but not on the same level as Scripture.

Recognize the Real

Don't believe everything you hear. Carefully weigh and examine what people tell you. The Secret Service is in charge of more than protecting politicians or the president; they also check our money supply to make sure it is not counterfeit. Do you know how they train to spot counterfeit money? They study and know what a real bill looks like. That way, when they come in contact with fake money, they recognize that it is not the real thing.

Focus on God's Agenda

What does it mean to take ownership of your life? What does it mean to no longer be a victim and no longer blame circumstances and people for all the problems in your life? What does it mean to realize that God has a plan for your life? In alignment with His Word, you don't have to live a stressed-out life. God has a plan and a purpose for your life. In alignment with His Word, you can reshape every thought that has formed a false belief that brings you down. God's Word can change your thinking and renew your mind to develop new beliefs.

When we are immersed in culture, we can quickly drift away from the truth of God's Word. The truth about who we are and where we are going is found in Scripture. We call it the God agenda. It simply takes the messages written on our hearts by media, movies, music and culture and filters them through God's Word. It identifies and corrects the messages of the heart.

The Scriptures call us to be separate from the world, not isolated from it. How do we do that? We live in culture while guarded and filtered through God's agenda.

While your expectations have been shaped by the parenting style and the culture you knew while growing up, you're also influenced by something else: your personality! In the next chapter, we're going to look at the four types of personalities and how understanding your personality and your mate's can result in a healthier marriage and expectations for both of you that are based in reality.

FROM GARYSMALLEY.COM

This question was sent to our website by a woman who is at her wit's end when it comes to debt and the deterioration of her marriage.

Q: In over 15 years of marriage, my husband and I have never been on the same page when it comes to money. We are both stressed out over credit card debt. He believes that debt is sinful, and until we get out of debt, God will not bless us. I don't go that far. We have made mistakes when it comes to money, but I don't want this debt to destroy our marriage. Any advice?

A: Not knowing every detail of your situation, I do know this: Most couples accumulate large credit card debt due to spending more than what they earn. High expectations for living can put a couple in serious trouble.

My greatest encouragement to you is to find a page that you and your husband can both read at the same time and solve this debt problem together. You both have deep beliefs about money that are driving every word you speak and every action you take. These beliefs have been shaped from your parents and from the culture around you. Study the Scriptures together to bring your beliefs about money into alignment with God's principles.

Take a look at these Scripture passages, and for the next week, discuss a passage a day:

- *Avoid borrowing whenever possible.* "The rich rule over the poor, and the borrower is servant to the lender" (Prov. 22:7).

- *Make sure that your use of credit is not replacing your trust in God's timing.* "Be still before the Lord and wait patiently for him; do not fret when men succeed in their ways, when they carry out their wicked schemes" (Ps. 37:7).

- *Avoid credit when buying wants, not needs.* Be content. "I am not saying this because I am in need, for I have learned to be content whatever the circumstances" (Phil. 4:11). "But godliness with contentment is great gain. For we brought nothing into the world, and we can take nothing out of it. But if we have food and clothing, we will be content with that" (1 Tim. 6:6-8).

- *Pay your debts on time.* "The wicked borrow and do not repay, but the righteous give generously" (Ps. 37:21).

- *If you are unable to make your payments, make arrangements with the credit card companies.* "My son, if you have put up security for your neighbor, if you have struck hands in pledge for another, if you have been trapped by what you said, ensnared by the words of your mouth, then do this, my son, to free yourself, since you have fallen into your neighbor's hands: Go and humble yourself; press your plea with your neighbor!" (Prov. 6:1-3).

Debt is stressful. I know the strain it can put on a couple. You and your husband need to be a team and make a plan together. Get help through Christian financial counseling and debt consolidation. Blessings on you as you work at this together.

CHAPTER 4

PERSONALITY PLAY

Norma and I (Gary) are opposite in just about every way. We view life through very different lenses. Our personalities fuel marital expectations that are both good and bad.

This past year, I was invited to be part of one of the most exciting ministries ever initiated for saving marriages worldwide. Large corporations and donors got together and launched the Marriage and Family Foundation in an effort to bring back the value of marriage to America. This group asked Norma and me to serve as trustees. My personality instantly embraces new "huge" opportunities. I am constantly looking for the next big possibility. My staff is often amazed at me because they think it is impossible for me to see the drawbacks or shortcomings of an idea or new concept. I am a greenlight thinker and struggle at times with people I perceive as overly cautious.

Thankfully, God brought a wonderful woman into my life who has a very different personality from mine. Norma did not jump for joy with the invitation we received.

"What are their expectations of a trustee?" Norma asked.

"I don't know, but we can find out," I said.

"We've got a lot to figure out before we accept this position. We need to talk to our accountant and attorney to see how to proceed with this," Norma said. She had a list of other questions that needed to be answered and we did not accept this new opportunity until they were all sufficiently addressed. It took over a month for us to make this decision. While the process was frustrating to me, it has reminded me why Norma is so valuable in my life.

Through the years, I frequently saw Norma's questions as roadblocks to what I thought God wanted to accomplish in our ministry. Norma viewed her questions as precautions that kept me out of jail or bankruptcy.

The way Norma and I face our major decisions in life flows straight from the core of who we are—from our personalities.

The issue of personality differences is a favorite for both Ted and me. We have seen throughout the years how understanding your own personality as well as those around you can improve marriages, relationships and quality of life on every level. That's why we're going to give you a detailed breakdown of the four common personality types. Then, we're going to give you four ways to reconcile any unhealthy expectations or differences you brought into your marriage. We believe this chapter can and will revitalize your marriage.

Opposites Attract

Did you marry someone who is very different from you? Odds are that you did! There's a lot of truth to the old adage that opposites attract. Because your personality is different from your spouse's, you probably approach and respond to situations and people in a different way than your spouse does. That's why it's so important to understand personalities—not just your own, but also your spouse's. When you understand the way you're both wired, you are less likely to cross wires and cause hurtful issues in your marriage!

If you've been experiencing conflict or frustration in your marriage, it's a direct result of not understanding how God made your spouse. That's why in this chapter we're going to explore four basic personality types and examine how understanding the differences in personalities can help bring your expectations into line in all your relationships.

The Precise Personality
(also called the Beaver Personality)

The Precise Personality loves to analyze. This person pays attention to statistics. Precise Personalities enjoy keeping a budget and balancing the checkbook. They love measuring and comparing things. For the Precise Personality, most issues are clearly black or white. The Precise Personality

PRECISE PERSONALITY	
Relational Strengths:	Accuracy and precision Assures quality control Discerning Analytical
Strengths Out of Balance:	Too critical or too strict Too controlling Too negative of new opportunities Loses overview
Communication Style:	Factual Two-way Great listener (tasks) Weakness: Desire for detail and precision can frustrate others
Relational Needs:	Quality Exact expectations
Relational Balance:	Total support is not always possible Thorough explanation isn't every- thing

is constantly evaluating incoming data. They'll happily tell you what you've done wrong and how you can do it better.

The world is a better place because of Precise Personalities. They make sure there is order in life. They make sure the guardrails are in place so people don't hurt each other. Precise personalities make sure that organizations run effectively and efficiently.

My wife, Norma, has a precise personality. She naturally expects that we will always do things the right way at the right time. I love this about her—except for those moments when I go to the ATM and forget to grab the receipt. Or when she schedules dinner with friends and I decide to replace the brakes on the car at the last minute—making us late! Or when she carefully organizes the closet and I haphazardly throw my things in.

Years ago, we were audited by the IRS for the first time, and Norma got all excited. You know why? She was convinced that after all the scrutiny was done, they would award her a blue ribbon. I love that about her! Precise Personalities tend to love order, structure and timeliness.

Norma doesn't like to admit this, but she is energized and excited after a two-hour phone call with American Airlines to organize our next trip. I really couldn't do ministry without her! Because I am the dreamer and Norma is the dream maker, we do function as a well-oiled machine. Together we can accomplish so much more than we could apart. But it's important to add that it can take a few hours or days to start the machine with each new project we do together. We accept and honor each other's differences, but it can certainly become too slow for me getting started up. She wants to wait until all of the "ducks" are lined up. And the one who decides how many ducks are necessary in the first place is . . . Norma.

The Precise Personality has many strengths. They tend to be detailed, accurate, analytical and sensitive. They are generally great with numbers; they are great with keeping your company, your organization, your church, your family on task.

PRECISE PERSONALITY EXPECTATIONS

LET'S DO EVERYTHING RIGHT AND IN ORDER
LET'S BE ON TIME TO APPOINTMENTS AND FAMILY EVENTS
GIVE ME ALL THE DETAILS IN THE CONVERSATION
DON'T LIE ABOUT THE FACTS (*I JUST SAY I'M LEAVING OUT
SOME DETAILS SO THE STORY IS MORE INTERESTING*)

There are areas in which you can get out of balance with this personality. The Precise Personality can become a perfectionist or become driven by doing everything so well that he or she never moves forward on decisions, creating "paralysis by analysis."

Getting along with the Precise Personality: Recognize that they just want you to honor all of their questions. They want you to answer them in the most detail possible. Honoring detail builds intimacy in a marriage with the Precise Personality. Going the extra mile to complete a project the "right" way says "I value you" to your mate.

Getting along if you're the Precise Personality: Remember that you may have to move forward without having everything figured out perfectly. You may need to complete the project or household chore even though it's not perfect. Even when it feels uncomfortable, you need to risk or embrace adventure. Do not expect your spouse to share every detail of the day. And by all means, he or she is not lying when details get left unsaid. Stretch yourself by not taking yourself or life too seriously.

The Pleaser Personality
(also known as the Golden Retriever)

The Pleaser Personality is warm and relational and tends to be extremely loyal. This personality maintains a sense of calm in the most stressful of situations and has a knack for being a natural peacemaker. The Pleaser Personality is often concerned with group dynamics and the atmosphere of the room. More than anything, he or she wants to make sure everyone and everything is good.

The world is a better place because of Pleaser Personalities. They tend to be the ones who are the glue that hold people and organizations together. They are quick to welcome, serve and embrace others. Without Pleaser Personalities, it would be hard to build a strong community.

My wife, Amy, exhibits many traits of the Pleaser Personality. She is a natural servant and loves people. She's warm, relational and impressively loyal. I know she has my back at every turn. In addition, she is extremely sensitive to make sure everyone feels like they're a part of whatever we're doing.

PLEASER PERSONALITY	
Relational Strengths:	Warm and relational Loyal Enjoys routine Peacemaker Sensitive to others feelings Attracts the hurting
Strengths Out of Balance:	Missed opportunities Stays in a rut Sacrifices own feelings for harmony Easily hurt or holds a grudge Indirect Two-way
Communication Style:	Great listener Weakness: Uses too many words or provides too many details Emotional security
Relational Needs:	Agreeable environment Learn to say no—establish emotional boundaries
Relational Balance:	Learn to confront when your feel- ings are hurt

Holidays and family are synonymous around the Cunningham home. Year after year, Amy rises to the occasion and overwhelms us with her ability to make every person feel extra special. My wife knows how to throw great parties. I love watching The Food Network stars Rachel Ray and Paula Deen, but I think my wife blows them both out of the water when it comes to hospitality. Whether we have 2 or 20 people over for a party, my wife always ends the night by asking me this simple question: "Do you think everyone had a good time?" She wants to make sure that bonding took place and everyone felt connected and special.

The theme of Amy's life is "Let's do this together!" When it comes to a task, the Precise Personality will make sure the job gets done right and on time. The Pleaser Personality will not focus on the job as much as the relational aspect and making sure everyone is a part of the task. The Pleaser Personality wants everyone to feel part of the team.

PLEASER PERSONALITY EXPECTATIONS
LET'S DO EVERYTHING TOGETHER
LET'S MEET EACH OTHER'S NEEDS
LET'S HAVE PLENTY OF CONVERSATIONS
LET'S STAY IN HARMONY

One of the struggles of people who have the Pleaser Personality is that they can inadvertently wear their heart on their sleeve. Because they care so much about relationships, they can get emotionally over involved. They usually need time to go home and mull things over and then will return, asking, "What exactly did you mean by that?" The Pleaser Personality is so concerned with others that they tend to second-guess their responses as well as others.

My wife gets worn out on Sunday morning, and do you know why? The Pleaser Personality likes to have a few relationships that go very deep. She cannot stand to have a hundred 30-second conversations on Sunday morning. She prefers deeper conversations and is concerned that she can't do that with everyone.

Getting along with the Pleaser Personality: Be cautious of their feelings. They can be taken advantage of easily, so work at valuing their loyalty. If your spouse does not embrace all of your friends, it's not because she or he thinks your friends are bad people. They prefer to go deep with fewer people instead of going shallow with a lot of people. Don't expect them to be a party mixer. Invite them to join you for dinner dates with associates rather than always going to the large group gatherings.

Getting along if you're the Pleaser Personality: You must be careful not to wear your heart on your sleeve. People, including your mate, may take advantage of that. Release past hurts. Let your spouse off the hook for past mistakes. Learn to make decisions in the midst of uncertainty about what is best for everyone. Branch out and meet new people.

The Party Personality
(also known as the Otter)

Ah, the best personality. Just kidding. This is my (Gary's) personality. The party personality is all about fun. We are going to have a ball. The Party Personality will cheer you on. If you think something is not such a good idea, just call a Party Personality. They'll tell you, "That's the most brilliant thing I have ever heard in my life!"

The Party Personality is always on the go. They're ready to try a new sport, jump out of a plane or catch a concert—at the last minute. Along the way, they'll make sure the laughter is loud and everyone gets to hear some of their best stories.

Those with the Party Personality are often daydreamers. They're constantly imagining what could be as well as how much fun it could be! They tend to come up with great ideas and love to be spontaneous.

Unfortunately, as enjoyable as the Party Personality is to be around, they also have their blind spots—like when it comes to doing the work needed to throw the party. Although they may love to be the center of attention at the party, that doesn't mean they should be the ones to throw the party! Their organizational skills leave much to be desired. All their excitement can lead to an overbearing presence. While they have a lot to say when it comes to making a decision, they may

PARTY PERSONALITY	
Relational Strengths:	Optimistic Energetic Motivators Future oriented
Strengths Out of Balance:	Unrealistic or daydreamer Impatient or overbearing Manipulative or pushy Avoids details or lacks follow- through.
Communication Style:	Can inspire others Optimistic or enthusiastic One-way Weakness: High energy can manipu- late others Approval
Relational Needs:	Opportunity to verbalize Visibility Social recognition Be attentive to mate's needs
Relational Balance:	There is such a thing as too much optimism

be too busy having fun to actually be a part of following through on that decision.

The Precise Personality wants to get things done right. The Pleaser Personality wants to get things done together. The Party Personality wants to make sure that everyone is having fun.

PARTY PERSONALITY EXPECTATIONS

LET'S HAVE FUN WITH WHATEVER WE ARE DOING

LET'S NOT TO BE TOO SERIOUS

WE MUST LEARN TO LAUGH AT OURSELVES

Getting along with the Party Personality: We could all stand to lighten up just a bit. The party personality reminds us to do just that. Avoid belittling this personality with constant words like, "Come on, get serious!" or "Why don't you ever take things seriously?" If your spouse is a Party Personality, then celebrate his or her motivation and visionary talents. Those are some powerful factors of a great home. Don't stifle a Party Personality's creativity. Give them room to explore new ideas and projects.

Getting along if you're the Party Personality: Learn to follow through on your ideas and especially your commitments. If you go to Lowe's and buy tools to do a project around the house, do the project. If you don't follow through, you'll drive the Precise Personality nuts and frustrate the Powerful Personality. Remember: Just because the fun leaves the project doesn't mean the project is over.

The Powerful Personality
(also known as the Lion)

The Powerful Personality loves making decisions. They are naturally task-oriented and focus on getting things done. This is my (Ted's) personality. Powerful Personalities naturally step up to leadership opportunities. They're quick to take the reins of a project or activity. They aren't afraid of competition or confrontation.

The Powerful Personality tends to look at relationships as *I'm your coach, not your friend.* They tend to have high expectations of themselves and others. They are not afraid to speak up, and they're willing to do what it takes to make sure the job gets done.

If left unchecked, the Powerful Personality has a natural tendency to think, *It's my way or the highway.* As a result, they can undermine relationships within a community or working environment. If a Powerful Personality gets out of balance, they may use their gung-ho leadership

POWERFUL PERSONALITY	
Relational Strengths:	Takes charge Problem solver Competitive Enjoys change Confrontational
Strengths Out of Balance:	Too direct or impatient Too busy Cold blooded Impulsive or takes big risks Insensitive to others
Communication Style:	Direct or blunt One-way Weakness: Not always a good listener
Relational Needs:	Personal attention and recognition for what they do Areas where he or she can be in charge Opportunity to solve problems Freedom to change Challenging activities Add softness
Relational Balance:	Become a great listener

skills to mow over or intimidate others. The result can be a lot of relational damage.

Precise Personalities thrive during extended boardroom meetings. They are satisfied when their schedule is filled with short, timely meetings. The Pleaser Personality likes groups to be smaller; they tend to be more introverted. The Party Personality is convinced that the more people the merrier! The Powerful Personality is the only personality that doesn't get along with itself. If you put two Powerful Personalities in a cage, we joke that only one will come out alive.

POWERFUL PERSONALITY EXPECTATIONS

LET'S GET IT DONE

LET'S DO IT MY WAY

GIVE ME JUST ENOUGH DETAILS

IN THE CONVERSATION

Getting along with the Powerful Personality: If you're a Powerful Personality yourself, then you need to make room for others to work together effectively. If you're married to another Powerful Personality, then we highly encourage you to get counseling; you're a "war" waiting to happen. Effective counseling will pay off for years to come as you learn to live together patiently, become great listeners and learn to soften any dogmatism. If you do this, as a couple you really can change the world together! This personality type loves loyalty. Anything you can say or do that expresses "I am on your side" or "I am on your team" builds trust. When asking questions of the Powerful Personality, approach from the perspective of "I want to understand," not "I want to be in control."

Getting along if you're the Powerful Personality: Add balance to your personality by adding softness. Study ways to become a better listener. Learn that not every statement needs a response. Tame your words with love and your tone with gentleness. Look for opportunities to take other people's feelings into account.

Personality Play in Marriage

Personality may or may not be a big issue in your marriage. For Norma and me, personality does come into play, especially in our ministry. Some of our strongest conflicts have taken place at our company, the Smalley Relationship Center (SRC). I speak for SRC, but Norma runs the business side of the ministry.

Whenever we call a staff meeting, there is always a great potential for disaster. Here's why: At the first sign that something isn't well received, I want to can the project and start dreaming up a new and improved idea. That's what Party Personalities do. They think if something isn't working then they can just fix it by trying something else. After all, the new project will be more exciting and fun!

Meanwhile, Norma comes into the meeting with a completely different perspective. As a Precise Personality, she's naturally armed with spreadsheets, calendars and minutes from the last meeting. She reminds me what projects we committed to last week and asks that we keep heading down that road. After all, books cannot be published in a week, and events take longer than one or two days to plan.

Do you see the unmet expectations that can arise between a Party Personality and a Precise Personality to cause conflict? That's why it's so important that Norma and I are intentional about our relationship and look for ways to resolve differences and seek compromise. Of course, with my personality, I naturally love it. Sounds like a party to me!

Personality is not really an issue for Amy and me in our marriage. That doesn't mean we don't have lots of other issues to work on, like the parent gap and generational struggles, but we naturally get along well. Do you want to know our secret? The Powerful Personality and the Pleaser Personality are naturally the least conflicted blend of all the personalities.

By nature, Pleaser Personalities are die-hard loyal to the Powerful Personalities. And the Powerful Personalities desire loyalty to those we relate to—so it's a beautiful combination.

When Amy and I want to grab a bite to eat, I'll ask her where she wants to go. Only once in a blue moon will she have a strong opinion. She's happy with anything. The only time she really disagrees is when we're heading to the same restaurant for the twelfth consecutive time. She reminds me that we're falling into a rut, and I need that reminder!

Here are a couple of things to note about personalities. First, most people tend to be a blend of two or more personality types. They may have one predominant personality trait, but it's usually combined with a second one. Second, no matter what personality combination you have in your marriage, you can learn the skills you need to enjoy a happy, fruitful and satisfying marriage.

Resolving Personality Expectations

So how do you learn to improve your relationship with your spouse and resolve personality expectations? Here are four important and practical things you can do.

1. Accept the Personality Difference

Realize that you are truly different from your spouse—and that's a good thing! Take a moment to read through the words of Psalm 139:13-16 concerning yourself:

> For you created my inmost being; you knit me together in my mother's womb. I praise you because I am fearfully and wonderfully made; your works are wonderful, I know that full well. My frame was not hidden from you when I was made in the secret place. When I was woven together in the depths of the earth, your eyes saw my unformed body. All the days ordained for me were written in your book before one of them came to be.

Now read that a second time in regard to your spouse. Psalm 139 isn't just about you—it's about your mate, your children, your parents, your in-laws, your coworkers and everyone else you know. When you honor and esteem someone as a unique creation and highly valuable, you cannot help but transform the relationship.

Honoring someone is simply seeing him or her as personally auto-graphed by God. Romans 15:7 says, "Accept one another, then, just as Christ accepted you, in order to bring praise to God." In other words, God is pleased when you honor others!

That means that based on your personality, when you get involved with another person or group, it doesn't always have to be your way or the highway. When you get involved, it doesn't always have to be fun. When you get involved, you may have to make a decision and move forward even if you don't know every last detail. And when you get involved, you may need to wrap up the project because of a deadline before everyone has developed deep, meaningful relationships with each other.

2. Avoid Judging or Criticizing Personality Differences

It's easy to look at a personality that's different from your own and find fault with it.

For me, I (Gary) often tend to be shortsighted. I'm tempted to think, God, You have given me a great personality. Who doesn't love having fun? Who doesn't love laughter? If everyone were more lighthearted like me, then we'd get along so much better.

That kind of thinking is self-centered and arrogant. It places me in a posture where I'm looking at what other people don't have instead of what they do! That's one reason that Romans 14:13 challenges, "Therefore let us stop passing judgment on one another." Instead of looking for what's wrong with each other, we need to look for what's right!

In a marriage, that means making sure that we don't shut down a conversation prematurely because our mind is made up. That means not closing our spirit to our spouse and turning away without fully seeking a solution. And that means taking the time to listen to and understand what the other person is communicating in his or her words, actions, tone and attitude.

During your next conflict, you may be tempted to lash out at your spouse about a particular personality weakness or tendency. Instead, focus your energy on finding your spouse's strengths. Gently remind your spouse that you're on the same team, you're committed to the marriage and you love her/him—right where he or she is!

3. Allow for Misunderstandings and Trial and Error

Even the best marriages have misunderstandings. There are moments when communication fails and frustration follows. The tension that results can be compounded by personality differences. But if you take a step back and learn to listen and love each other, then you will grow closer together over time.

Learning to celebrate personality differences takes time. It doesn't happen overnight. And it will require trial-and-error attempts at growing closer. You may think you're doing something your spouse would love—when in fact it's driving your spouse nuts! Those moments will become scrapbook memories that will provide lots of laughter for years to come (though it probably isn't funny right now).

4. Look for Balance

Ephesians 4:2 tells us, "Be completely humble and gentle; be patient, bearing with one another in love." When you practice that verse in a marriage, your relationship cannot help but grow stronger. At the same time, you'll find the gap between your personalities shrinking as you learn to love each other more deeply.

I (Ted) want to work every day to bring balance to my personality. I don't want it to be out of balance. I don't want to be known as someone who is pushy, obnoxious, demanding. I don't want to be a bad listener. I don't want a personality that comes across as arrogant or cocky. Who wants that label? No one! That's why we need to learn to bring balance—to grow in humility, gentleness, patience and love. In fact, when the fruit of the Spirit is nurtured in our life, we can't help but become more balanced and gracious to others.

Now that we've looked at three areas of discovery in regard to expectations, including parenting style, cultural influences and personality play, there's one more area you need to consider: *your past baggage*. In the next chapter, we're going to help you unpack some of the boxes of your previous relationships. In addition to reflecting on your previous dating relationships, we want to provide practical help for blended families. That's why we're including six tips we call getting the "Best of the Blend." Whether you're on your first marriage or a subsequent marriage, this is a chapter you can't afford to miss.

FROM GARYSMALLEY.COM

This question was sent to our website by a man struggling with feelings that his wife is always correcting and criticizing him.

Q: My wife is trying to be my mom. She nitpicks every little thing I do. How can I make her stop?

A: All of us have distinct personalities, and all of us can, without knowing it, push some of our inborn characteristics to an unhealthy extreme that can wreak havoc in a marriage.

It used to really get to me when my wife corrected my driving. I told her time and again to cut it out, but to no avail. I used to believe that she did it just to ruin my day. It got to the point where I sulked and clammed up every time we rode anywhere. But now I realize the reason. She almost died in a serious auto accident in high school—losing two of her good friends. When she thinks I'm veering too close to the edge of the road, she is simply reliving that terrible night.

This realization caused me to change my thinking. I realized that she isn't the one making me unhappy when she gets upset at my driving; I make myself unhappy with my prideful reaction to her criticism. I decided to understand the lingering trauma of her experience and show compassion and care for her. I admit that sometimes her criticism still gets under my skin a little, but now I use even this minor irritation as a spur to growth. I have even started thanking her because God uses her comments to increase my patience and thus deepen my maturity with Him.

You have the freedom and responsibility to change yourself, but you have neither the freedom nor the responsibility to change another person, not even your mate. If you fail to grasp this principle and try to hold yourself responsible for changing your spouse, you will inevitably fail. Your failure may lead to anger, despair, hopelessness or even guilt. When you experience the urge to blame, remember King Solomon's wise words: "A man of knowledge uses words with restraint, and a man of understanding is even-tempered" (Prov. 17:27).

Perhaps the worst thing about attempting to change your mate is that those attempts create an unsafe place for your marriage to thrive. And in time, your mate will erect walls to ward off your continued push toward change. Trying to change your mate can only make your marriage worse and increase its chance of failure.

Are there any areas in your wife's past history—a role model in her family of origin or perhaps a personality strength that is a little bit out of balance right now and needs some loving attention from you? Think about her primary needs, such as to do things with you as a team, or to see you be a person who follows through on projects. When you understand her basic emotional needs, you can begin to react differently to her unwanted behavior, which in turn may result in different behavior from her.

Ultimately, you only have the freedom and responsibility to change yourself and how you react.

CHAPTER 5

PAST RELATIONSHIPS

After five marriages, she still felt empty and unfulfilled. She found her-self quietly disappointed with guy number six. She convinced herself that things couldn't get better—that they wouldn't get better. Why tie the knot? She thought. We'll just live together and see how it goes.

Oh, how Jesus loved that lady! What did the Son of God say to a woman who had been married five times and had moved on to guy number six?

Jesus answered, "Everyone who drinks this water will be thirsty again, but whoever drinks the water I give him will never thirst. Indeed, the water I give him will become in him a spring of water welling up to eternal life."

The woman said to him, "Sir, give me this water so that I won't get thirsty and have to keep coming here to draw water."

He told her, "Go, call your husband and come back."

"I have no husband," she replied.

Jesus said to her, "You are right when you say you have no husband. The fact is, you have had five husbands, and the man you now have is not your husband. What you have just said is quite true" (see John 4:13-18).

While reading this story, Don resonated with the passage in a way that caught him off guard. He had been married four times and was cur-rently living with a woman. After saying "I do" so many times and only experiencing disappointment, Don's expectations for marriage were at rock bottom.

When I met Don, he was considering marrying the woman he was living with. In his mid-fifties, he had fathered four children with two different wives. None of his children wanted anything to do with him.

Though he always kept up on alimony and child support payments, he didn't have a healthy relationship with any of his kids or previous wives. As I listened to his story, my knee-jerk reaction was to prescribe celibacy for life. I quietly wondered how someone who had been through so much could possibly change. But that's when I remembered the power of God and Christ to transform someone from the inside out.

I had the privilege of watching God be God in Don's life. He became a follower of Jesus at our church, and when he made that commitment, he was ready to serve God with everything he had. Knowing his desire for God, I counseled him through a journey that some might consider impractical, ungracious and sexually impossible. I'll never forget that breakfast at a Bob Evans restaurant.

"Ted, there is no way I can go without sex!" Don said. "And Scripture itself says that if you burn with lust, marriage is the only outlet for it."

"Don, you are speaking truth, but you are not speaking all of the truth," I answered. "Marriage is far more than just an outlet for sex. It is also about caring for your spouse for a lifetime. I know you are a new believer, and God has covered your previous marriages, but if I may be blunt, you are not ready to marry number five. You need to begin the journey of following Christ alone. I want to challenge you to begin growing as a Christ follower without the impeding presence of someone who is not a believer.

"How long has it been since your last divorce?" I pressed.

"Last year," Don said, revealing a reserved, defeated look.

"Don, I say this because I love you and want the absolute best for you. But you are not ready for remarriage. You still have much healing to do. And part of your healing involves your expectations. Right now, as a new follower of Jesus, you do not even have the expectation that your girlfriend will become a Christian. That is a critical expectation that you must have."

Don sat silent. I knew we were starting to peel back the layers of an onion that would reveal his low expectations.

"Why would a Christian woman want to marry me?" Don asked.

"It is not about whether or not a Christian woman would want to marry you, but more about what kind of Christian man you are going to become. I have high hopes that my daughter, Corynn, will marry a strong man of God. What I am teaching her is that she does not need to be on the prowl for a godly man to marry, but rather she needs to work on becoming a godly woman. After all, we attract what we become. Don, you have a low image of who you are in Christ. We need to work on who you are and can become in Christ. And if marriage enters the picture down the road, so be it."

My friend Don needed a period of time where his journey with the Lord was the priority. Jesus did not offer the woman at the well marital advice; He offered Himself—the Living Water. In that day, the rabbis permitted a person to divorce two to three times. Beyond that was excessive. Jesus did not address any of that. He went straight to the real need. He was the only solution for that woman.

As I told my friend Don, "You are not at a place to give your heart to another woman. I know young people marry for the first time with no marital skills and they just kind of work it out and learn as they go. But they also do not have the baggage from previous marriages. Before you pursue another relationship, you need to take time to heal from your previous relationships."

I am thrilled to report that within a week, Don moved out of his living situation. He threw himself into his work, his church and serving others. Before Don's decision to find and follow Christ, he had the strong belief that a wife or live-in woman was what he needed to be happy. He couldn't even imagine himself celibate; and if there was no sex, he'd never be happy. Once he started his new belief that Christ alone can make him not only happy but also complete and overflowing with love for others and himself, he started his new journey in discovering how complete Christ is in Himself. He soon joined Celebrate Recovery at our church and now has loving believers in his life to help him on his journey. I would not rule out the possibility of marriage for Don down the road. But for now, he loves the Lord and his life.

Now that we've looked at how parenting styles, cultural influences and personality influence the expectations you bring into marriage, it's time to look at the final factor: your previous relationships. We're going to challenge you to unpack your dating years and previous relationships to see how the past has shaped the way you view and respond to your current marriage relationship. If you're in a blended family, you're going to discover six tips for getting the "Best of the Blend."

You just may discover that your past relationships are affecting you more than you realize!

Unpacking the Dating Years

Two lines overheard at a popular single's club:

> "I've been looking for Mr. Right. Now I'm looking for Mr.
> Pretty Good."
> "Oh no, he's really not Mr. Right—but he is Mr. Right Now."

You may still be unpacking boxes from previous dating relationships. For some people, dating is a healthy environment full of great experiences. You used your season of dating as an opportunity to develop strong social skills with the opposite sex. Your dates were primarily safe, platonic and fun.

For others, dating was not so pleasant. Maybe you lived in a town where the odds were good but the goods were odd. Or maybe you dated because of parental or peer pressure. Maybe you looked at the calendar and began dating because you felt time was passing you by. Dating can be hard on anyone. Maybe you had your heart crushed, your thoughts about a healthy relationship scrambled. Maybe your dating relationships were unhealthy, inappropriately intimate or ended with heartache.

I (Ted) am a huge proponent of dating. I appreciate Joshua Harris and his perspective in the book *I Kissed Dating Goodbye*, but I can think of many positive and healthy couples that dated well without succumbing to the societal pressures of sex. Dating for all the right reasons is healthy and prepares young people for courting and marriage. I am all for "pressure free" dating. That is dating for fun with no pressure for a "romantic encounter" at the end of the evening.

But not all dating relationships are healthy ones. You may be carrying around boxes packed with bad, abusive or even dangerous dating relationships. If you dated without boundaries or were taken advantage of by someone you thought you would spend your lifetime with, you will need to take time to unpack those previous dating boxes and examine the expectations they created for your marriage.

Countless songs have been written about a person's high-school sweetheart, only to be disappointed later in life. One country singer expressed his thoughts in the chorus, "How do you like me now?" The male singer was the one a young woman had said no to in high school only later to watch him become a superstar.

For Ericka, it was more than the lyrics of a country song; it was her life. Rob was the top gun of their school. He had the attention of the girls, the teachers and the college recruiters. He was going places, and Ericka was on board. She loved him and described Rob as her "soul mate." That's one reason she finally gave in to his repeated requests for sex.

Though the dugout at the high school didn't seem like the right place to lose one's virginity, Ericka convinced herself that she was with the right guy. They continued to date throughout their senior year of high school but broke up in the middle of their first semester of college. Though not uncommon, the experience devastated Ericka. She carried the baggage from that one relationship into every other dating relationship and eventually into her marriage.

Ericka began to see herself as an object. She convinced herself that as long as she was giving herself to men, without question or reservation, then everything would be okay. She found her second "soul mate" in college. This guy was sexually aggressive. Plain sex only satisfied him for a couple of months. When he invited her to view pornography with him, she agreed. She thought she had to or else he would get bored with her and leave her.

She did not believe that she could do better, and with college graduation approaching, Ericka felt pressure to tie the knot. She rushed the engagement and made an unwise decision. Her first husband led her into a lifestyle of pornography, affairs and same-sex encounters. He pressured her to join him at every turn. Eventually, they filed for divorce.

I had the opportunity to counsel Ericka and her second husband, Marcus. I quickly noticed a big difference between Marcus and the other men Ericka had dated and even married. Marcus was neither a user nor abuser. He loved the Lord and was committed to raising a godly family. Ericka and Marcus allowed me the privilege of sitting down and unpacking the previous relationship box with both of them.

As we worked through the box, we addressed issues of abuse, sexual trauma, hurt, pain, loss, distrust, misplaced value of human life . . . and the list goes on. Lack of trust and worthlessness were at the bottom of the box.

Eventually we threw away the box and got them something new: a basket. A box is something you store things in. But a basket is something that goes with you and is filled with treats and delights. The first thing we placed in Ericka's basket was value. We needed her to know her value as a child of God. We needed her to know that she was priceless in God's eyes, someone to be treasured and celebrated.

Then we placed trust in Ericka's basket. She needed to learn to trust God. She needed to know that He was never going to leave her nor forsake her. God is trustworthy. And so was Marcus. She needed to grow in trust in all of her relationships.

Ericka committed Psalm 139:14-16 to memory: "Thank you for making me so wonderfully complex! Your workmanship is marvelous.... You watched me as I was being formed.... You saw me before I was born. Every day of my life was recorded in your book. Every moment was laid out before a single day had passed" (*NLT*).

As Ericka hid God's Word in her heart, she found her attitudes and reactions changing. She began to experience love from God and her husband like she had never experienced before. Along the way, she found new things in her basket—joy, hope and a peace she had never experienced before. She felt like one of the richest women on the planet!

As she has continued to grow in her relationship with God, she's come to believe that there's power in Philippians 4:8-9: "Whatever is true, whatever is noble, whatever is right, whatever is pure, whatever is lovely, whatever is admirable—if anything is excellent or praiseworthy—think about such things." She's discovered that when she focuses on these things, her perception changes.

At first, Ericka had such a low image of who she was in Christ that she could not handle Marcus treating her well. Marcus was treating her with the respect, gentleness and grace that he is called to; but because of Ericka's previous relationship box, she could not receive it.

Over time, she found herself not only embracing that love but discovering healing and restoration through it!

Steps to Unpacking the Previous Relationship Box

What have you packed and stored away in your "past relationships box"? If you were able to develop skills and emotional strength in past relationships so that you could forge a loving marriage, then thank God with all your heart. But if Ericka's story has any similarities with your own situation, especially in the area of self-worth and an understanding of how cherished God intends your life to be, then read on. We have some initial steps to help you sort through and throw out what you need to let go.

Unpack the Box with Help from Others

A trained counselor, pastor, trusted friend or small group may see things you don't. Like that old pair of shoes we have worn for years, a new set of eyes may see them and say something like, "Hey, I used to have a pair just like that," or "Wow, that takes me back in time, I remember those from the television commercials." Fresh perspective is always helpful.

Let Your Spouse Be a Part of the Unpacking

While you do not need to share every detail of where the item has been, you can share tidbits to allow your spouse to glean more insight into the expectations you brought with you.

Sort Through Your Expectations

Categorize your expectations as if you were getting ready for a garage sale. Some expectations you have brought into marriage are good. Others just need to be pitched or burned. For instance, some women get focused on the fact that all men are jerks and only want one thing. That would be one for the burn pile. You need a "This is true" pile and a "This is false" pile for sorting.

Don't Repack

One of my (Ted's) favorite things to do in counseling is to unexpectedly wipe everything off my desk in one fell swoop. It usually catches the couple off guard and has been known to freak some out. Some have even thought, *Ted's lost it. He finally went over the edge.* That's when I step in and explain forgiveness. When we forgive, it is a wiping clean by the blood of Jesus. Yet we humans, over a period of time, start picking things up one at a time and placing them back on the desk. That's what I mean by not repacking. When something comes out of the box, refuse to allow it back.

Next Time Around

The first time I (Ted) introduced the expectations assessment from chapter 1 to a group of couples, I was shocked by what I found. As I walked around the room, I noticed several couples with very low expectations (mostly under a 5 ranking). When I asked them why their expectations were so low, their answers were enlightening: "This is a second marriage for both of us."

Many relationship expectations come from first, second or even third marriages. A person leaves a marriage to start another and finds that he or she is no happier in the new one. With each marriage, expectations sink to a new low. Though many people think the next marriage will make them happier, they're actually degrading themselves in the process.

Harvard sociologist Armand Nicholi III concluded, "Divorce is not a solution, but an exchange of problems."[1] In a more personal way, novelist Pat Conroy said of his own marriage break-up, "Each divorce is the death of a small civilization."[2]

One woman wrote after her divorce, "Our divorce has been the most painful, horrid, ulcer producing, agonizing event you can imagine. . . . I wish I could put on this piece of paper for the entire world to see a picture of what divorce feels like. Maybe my picture would stop people before it's too late." *Psychology Today* noted that a whopping 60 percent of remarriages fail. And they do so even more quickly; after an average of 10 years, 37 percent of remarriages have dissolved versus 30 percent of first marriages.[3]

Unlike the previous four chapters, where we looked at how you brought lofty expectations into your marriage based on parents, generational differences, culture, movies, music and your personality, now you bring deflated expectations into your marriage.

Karen L. Maudlin, Psy.D., is a licensed clinical psychologist specializing in marriage and family therapy as well as a regular columnist for *Christian Parenting Today*. She writes:

> Couples entering a second marriage are often seen as lugging too much baggage to make a success of their next go-round. This assumes, however, that people can come into any relationship without baggage, or a history that impacts the relationship—an assumption that is, of course, untrue. Childhood, previous relationships, even relationships with siblings and friends over the course of life all impact spouse selection and the relationship that ensues from there onward.
>
> Second marriages are by nature more complicated and more at-risk for divorce than first marriages (over 60 percent divorce rate, compared to around 50 percent for first-time marriages). Yet it's also clear that remarriages need the same strong and consistent nurturing as first marriages. No matter what your stage of life or circumstance, with some extra TLC and effective communication, your second marriage can succeed.[4]

Here are some key considerations for the expectations you bring into a second marriage:

- Do not rush a second marriage or even dating.
- When it comes to healing from a previous marriage, think in terms of years, not weeks or months.
- See a marriage counselor before you start dating again. Gain perspective from your marital history. Unmet expectations from the first marriage will resurface in the next marriage.
- Offer forgiveness to your previous spouse. Unresolved anger will resurface in your next marriage.
- Be honest. When you begin dating again, don't "sugarcoat" the past. Share with each other your expectations, your hopes and your dreams.
- Don't beat yourself up on past mistakes. Focus on the future.

Now, you can imagine how the expectations are compounded when couples bring children into a second marriage. There are a host of expectations for second marriages when children are part of the package. Most expectations center around what kind of blended family you will shoot for.

There are four types of step-families:

1. The blended traditional family most resembles the traditional family and is the healthiest model. Both mom and dad understand that there needs to be open and honest communication between each other and the biological parents. Conversation over parenting styles is frank and includes the expectation that bonding as a family will take time. Tension and "side-taking" is limited because the husband and

wife (now in a second marriage) present a united front with the children.

2. The *blended idealistic family* lives with the idea that they will operate as a traditional family in short time. Two great expectations need to be resolved. First, the blended family will never be the traditional family. Second, even attempts to become a blended-traditional family will take time. The expectations of instant unity, cohesion, bliss and co-parenting leads to a large gap filled with stress.

3. The *blended matriarchal family* presents a home where mom is most definitely in charge and runs the show. Her husband follows her lead. She expects him to become a buddy to the children. He is to know of the whereabouts and the do's and don'ts of the child, but he is given clear limitations on discipline.

4. The *blended patriarchal family* presents a home where dad is the leader and runs the show. Mom follows his lead in most areas, but handles the discipline of her biological children. Much like the blended-matriarchal home, mom still expects her husband to be a buddy to the children.

Common expectations a spouse brings to the blended family:

- Cohesion and unity will take a little time, but once achieved, all will be bliss.
- We will coparent the children.
- We will love each other's children the same as our own.
- Favoritism will not exist in our home.

- As a couple, we will present a united front to the children. They will not be able to play us against each other.

Realistic expectations for all blended families:

- Cohesion and unity take time.
- The blended family will never be a traditional family.

Scott and Becca are well educated and devoted followers of Jesus. Blending a family has turned out to be the hardest thing they have ever done. They met at church and their relationship got off to a great start. They spent time reading books, attending seminars and listening to nationally known pastors during their dating and engagement. They felt adequately prepared for marriage since both of them were bringing in two children from their first marriages. They did not go into their second marriage with the idea that blending two families would be quick or easy. They both believed they had reasonable expectations entering their second marriage.

While loving each other came naturally and easily, co-parenting almost drove them apart.

Scott was raising two boys, and Becca was raising two girls. Scott grew up in a dominant home; Becca grew up in a firm and loving home. Therein lay the rub. Becca distanced herself, and the girls, from Scott every time he went to discipline them. They thought they started their marriage with realistic expectations and a strong parenting plan, but it wasn't long before the wheels started coming off the bus.

I met Scott and Becca shortly after their two-year anniversary. They were on the brink of divorce and had already started talking about it. In both their minds, now was a good time to end it. They had yet to purchase a home together, so that would make things easier financially. The boys and girls were not getting along well, so saying good-bye would be a relief. And they both had good jobs, so sustaining two homes was feasible.

Both Scott and Becca were functioning in "It's not my fault" mode. "If she would allow me to play a part in raising the girls, and not defend them every time I open my mouth, things would be a lot easier," Scott said.

"If he would lighten up around the house and stop acting like a drill sergeant running a military base, we could survive," Becca said.

While Scott and Becca discussed at great length the discipline around the home, neither of them thought through the emotions that would emerge as they watched someone else scold their child. Neither Scott nor Becca had the expectation of being a traditional family, but there were some strong emotional expectations under the surface for which neither was prepared.

Both Scott and Becca underestimated the parental bond. Even though it was unstated, both of them assumed they could love the other's child in the same way they loved their own. But reality was different. Becca had given birth to those girls and spent 10 years with one and 8 years with the other. That adds up to 10 Christmas trees, 18 birthday parties, several dozen school report cards and countless boo-boos that needed her comforting. The natural bond between immediate parent-child will always be stronger—for Becca and Scott.

Are Scott and Becca still together? Yes! While Scott and Becca navigated some choppy waters, I'm happy to inform you that they're still married eight years later. Here's how they did it.

Scott led his family on his own journey of personal responsibility. He knew that improving the quality of the relationship was more about his behavior around the home than it was anyone else's. By nature, Scott wanted to blame things on those in his home who upset him. It came under the guise of a messy room or back talking Mom or Dad. He worked hard to try to get his family to change how they treated him. He admits that along the way he tried some unhealthy ways to manipulate them and force their behavior to change. Every time, he ended up feeling hurt and frustrated.

For Scott to take personal responsibility meant that he refused to focus on what the other members of the family had done or were doing. He was tempted to think, *If only my stepdaughter would say this* or *If only my wife would support me in this*, but instead he began to focus on the transforming truth, *I can't change any of them, but I can change me.*

At first Scott's family was slow to acknowledge the change. They weren't sure if they were being manipulated. But then they began to realize that the change was real and it was here to stay.

Today, Scott and Becca are madly in love with each other and their family. As Scott demonstrated for his wife and kids what it looked like to take personal responsibility and choose to serve rather than be served, things fell into place in their relationship.

Scott embodies what this entire book is about. He brought truckloads of baggage into his marriage. He had hundreds of pounds of expectations in each suitcase. He spent some time unpacking, but in the end he decided to throw the luggage out. He is a beaming light for Christ Jesus. I am so proud of him. My friends Scott and Becca found the hope that comes only in Christ and personal responsibility.

In the next few chapters we're going to dive into a new part of the progression for healthy marriage: **personal responsibility.**

The Progression of a Healthy Marriage

Unmet Expectations ➻ Discovery ➻ Personal Responsibility ➻ **Commitment**

[chapter 1]   [chapters 2–5]   [chapters 6–8]   [chapters 9–11]

We're going to look at four keys to realigning your expectations as well as four principles to help you take personal responsibility for the expectations you bring into a marriage. This is a chapter you can't afford to miss.

Six Tips for Getting the "Best of the Blend"

Natalie Nichols Gillespie, author of *Stepfamily Success* and a resource member of the Stepfamily Steering Committee for the Association of Marriage and Family Ministries (AMFM), offers the following stepfamily advice:

1. Give Yourself Permission to Be Different

Stepfamilies are different from traditional, nuclear families. The sooner you give up the dream that your stepfamily will look "normal," the better. You have just taken a bunch of virtual strangers and put them together under one roof. You have no shared history, and it takes time to build one. It takes the average stepfamily two to five *years* to start feeling like a cohesive unit. So while "blended families" is a nice, warm fuzzy term, it's not usually accurate. Stepfamilies are more like oil and water. You can put everyone together and shake them up and they will blend for moments or even days, but they usually settle back into their original family loyalties and ways. They don't stay "blended." And that's absolutely normal and okay.

2. Put the Couple First

Stepfamilies must put the couple's relationship first. That can be a tall order for parents—because they had the kids before they had the new spouse. But the stepfamily is only as a strong as the couple's relationship. Children, especially children who have experienced their parents' divorce, desperately need the stability and positive example of a couple relationship that is solid. Make time for date nights, learn to resolve conflict in healthy ways and remain a united front. As a stepcouple, you will get pressure from all sides—from former spouses, financial challenges, and especially from the kids. Stand strong!

3. Let the Parent Be the "Bad" Guy in Discipline

In a stepfamily, the parent should administer the law, while the stepparent gives the grace. In most stepfamilies, the reverse is true. Stepparents—who missed their stepchildren's births, first words and adorable cuteness as an infant—tend to see more of the faults in their stepchildren. Parents, who have loved their children from day one, tend to be more lenient. This leads to tremendous conflicts in stepfamilies and must be reversed. Stepparents have not been in a position of influence with the children long enough to be the disciplinarians, and parents need to provide healthy boundaries for their children. The parent of the child should be the one who disciplines, while the stepparent takes the role of mentor or friend.

4. Avoid Trying to Force Love

Stepfamilies who find success take a relaxed approach to relationships. You can't expect stepsiblings to love each other or even like each other. And you don't have to feel guilty if you are not head over heels in love with your stepchildren right off the bat. You should require everyone to respect each other (and respect each other's personal property), but take a hands-off approach and let relationships in the stepfamily grow over time.

5. Compromise, Compromise, Compromise

Stepfamilies have to learn to compromise, and then compromise some more. If it brings peace to your family to have Christmas on December 21 or December 26 instead of the traditional December 25, change your traditions. Be willing to listen to each member of the stepfamily and allow everyone to have some input in holidays, family activities, summer plans and even discipline. Family meetings can be a great way for stepfamilies to work toward common goals. Allow children to have a say in what consequences should be levied for different offenses, and make the meetings a chance for everyone to talk about what positive changes can be made. Cherish the relationships that are building in your stepfamily more than being the one who is "right."

6. Be the One with the "Clean Hands"

In courtrooms, judges often say they are looking for the party with the "clean hands." That means the person who is operating from pure, honest intentions. In your stepfamily, make it your vow to be the one with the clean hands. Even if your former spouse is demanding and unreasonable, stay calm and keep the conflict away from your kids. Work daily on forgiveness, and practice peace. You cannot control the actions of those around you, but you can control your emotions, responses, and reactions. The next time a former spouse, stepchild or anyone in your stepfamily dynamic gets under your skin, remember Romans 12:18, "If it is possible, as far as it depends on you, live at peace with everyone."

FROM GARYSMALLEY.COM

This question was sent to our website by a man who is struggling with the issue of shared responsibility in achieving a healthy marriage relationship.

Q: How come it always seems to be the man who has to do all the work in a relationship? How come women are not told to learn about men, and how to communicate to their husbands? It seems to be all for the woman to have it the way she wants. Sounds very one-sided.

A: I think the simple answer is because men are asked to be leaders. We get to lead our families in how to communicate, learn from others and serve. When a man is truly seeking growth in his relationship with the Lord and his marriage, everybody wins.

In all of my years of counseling couples I have met very few women who did not respond to genuine effort and growth in their husband. Here's a little secret: Women have a built-in marriage manual. They know the difference between when a husband is doing the right things for the right reasons and when he is doing the right things for the purpose of getting his own way.

Many husbands make the mistake of waiting for their wife to change before they make a move toward change. Don't wait for your wife to change. You can start today by becoming a student of your wife. Don't worry about what she is learning or doing. You worry about your growth. Be the leader.

Now, if you are a wife, and your husband is not taking responsibility in your marriage, that doesn't let you off the hook.

Picture yourself walking around each day with a hula hoop around you. All day long you are in complete control of what takes place inside that hula hoop. You take control of you and your actions. First Peter

3:1-7 counsels that the more you grow in the Lord, the more gentle and quiet you will become. Your spiritual growth will produce peace and calm because you realize that you are not responsible for changing your husband. It is hard at first, but your growth in the Lord will naturally produce this calm. You will be relaxed, no longer harping on your husband to change. In turn, he may then take notice of this change and inquire as to what made the difference.

Marriage is in no way one-sided. It involves two people who are growing in the Lord. Each spouse must take 100 percent personal responsibility for his or her walk with the Lord.

EXPECT THE BEST

For the first 35 years of my life, I (Gary) thought people were supposed to make me happy. I had expectations of my family. I thought they were ready to lay down their lives, preferences and needs for the ministry of restoring marriage, just like I had. I'm embarrassed to admit that I had no problem expecting my wife and children to wait an hour outside in the cold until I finished a meeting or teaching session. I convinced myself that what I was doing was more important than loving and serving them.

Years passed before I realized that I had selfishly expected my wife and kids to serve my ambition. No wonder Norma and I weren't experiencing much joy in our marriage. Our relationship was lopsided.

All too often, I see this type of scenario play out between young couples. For instance, there's the woman who dreams for years about finding "Mr. Wonderful." She believes this man will fulfill her deepest longing for intimacy. She pictures him sitting next to her on an overstuffed love seat in front of a warm fire, talking for hours with his arm around her. She sees them discussing their plans for the future, their next vacation and how they'll redecorate the living room. She knows he will diligently fix things around the house, keep her car running smoothly and be there to support and encourage her when she's feeling discouraged. She often thinks of her husband-to-be as a waterfall cascading into her life, a never-ending source of fulfillment that will make her life overflow with meaning.

This woman doesn't know she's setting herself up for the very heartache she's trying to escape. It doesn't take long—usually no more than a few weeks into the marriage—to realize that her husband, in many ways, can't or won't cooperate with her expectations. The relationship she expected to bring her security may actually make her feel more insecure. Her husband may be the type who notices every attractive girl who walks by. He may be so wrapped up in his work that he shows little interest in her work or activities. Like me, he may expect her to lay down her own desires for his work, career or ministry. He may be too tired to fix her car or make necessary household repairs. Even his interest in touching her may seem to have only sexual motivation.

It's not too long until this woman, who once had so many dreams, begins to feel used and taken for granted. Some days she even feels more like a manager or maid than a celebrated wife. Not only is he not charging her battery, but his insensitivity has started to drain her emotional resources. If not corrected, she will eventually lose whatever amount of love, happiness and peace she had when she entered the marriage.

When her husband fails to meet her needs, she may think of an alternative: "If my husband isn't going to meet my needs, then I'll find it another way. I'll have a family. Children running around the house are just what I need to be fulfilled!" Soon after her baby is born, she discovers that children, rather than charging her battery, have an amazing capacity to short-circuit it.

A man also enters marriage with many expectations. He pictures how his wife will respond to him. Each day she will comment on how gifted he is as a lover, husband and father. Without question, she will prepare delicious meals every night and always respond warmly to his sexual desires. She will frequently ask him about his day and allow him time to decompress or spend time with the guys.

He, too, discovers that not only is she unable to charge his battery, but being around her produces a brownout. Like her, his insecurity increases, and he may begin to think he married the wrong person. He may even begin to look around for another woman he thinks will better meet his needs and become his ultimate "battery charger."

An affair for either spouse may well produce a momentary power spike, but it doesn't take long before there's a major power shortage as the spouse attempts to keep the affair a secret. Affairs are a lot easier to start than finish. Repairing the damage from an affair is like trying to rewire an entire house after it has been hit by lightning; all the circuits are blown and the wires are melted.

Husbands and wives are by no means unique here. Everyone experiences frustration when they look to people to fulfill their expectations. Children may long for greater love from and better communication with their parents. Parents may feel like they've been taken advantage of by their children. Employees often feel that employers do not care about them as people. Employers may feel that employees have no sense of loyalty or gratitude. And many Christians feel betrayed when certain leaders succumb to temptation and turn out to be just as human and prone to failure as anyone else.

In the book of Proverbs, we read, "Hope deferred makes the heart sick" (Prov. 13:12). Many husbands, wives, children, friends, employees and employers put their hopes for fulfillment in other people, which eventually leaves them empty and frustrated inside.

This codependence creates the expectation in us that others are responsible for our fulfillment. When people let us down, life is bad. When people support us, life is good. God gives us relationships to *enrich* our lives, but not to *be* our lives.

I am grateful that I finally began to discover this principle, because my unrealistic expectations of others kept me from gaining the fulfillment I was desperately seeking. No matter how wonderful the people in my life may be, they will never be able to charge my life battery to full. When you place your expectations on other people and other things on this earth to fill you up, you will always be somewhat disappointed. And by "filling up" we mean really happy—feeling that alive emotion that comes from imagining gaining the right amount of material goods, the right number of people to love you and to love and the right amount of pleasure from doing the right number of thrilling activities in life. It's just not going to happen for you, and the sooner you realize it, the sooner you can discover what does, in fact, fill humans up to all the fullness of life and love.

We began this book by examining the issue of unmet expectations. Throughout the last few chapters, we've been on a journey of discovery to recognize issues that shape the expectations we bring into marriage. Now it's time to delve into one of the most crucial stages: taking *personal responsibility*.

In the next few pages, we want to give you four keys to help you realign your expectations, as well as four principles to help you take personal responsibility for the expectations you bring into a marriage.

Four Key Steps to Realign Your Expectations

Try to think of your expectations, for a moment, as furniture in the living room of your mind. What do you see there? Too many pieces of furniture? Pieces that are mismatched or uncomfortable? What needs to go? What can you keep? Before you can live well and comfortably in a fulfilling marriage, you need to take stock of the furniture you've arranged in your mind in the form of your expectations of what marriage would do for you. Then you can begin to realign those expectations in a more harmonious configuration.

1. Bring Your Expectations to the Surface

Start by making a list of the expectations you brought to your marriage or that you still have for your marriage that show the widest gap between expectation and reality. Then answer the following three questions for each expectation:

1. Do you need to change or adjust this expectation?
2. Is your expectation fair and reasonable?
3. If you express your expectation, will your spouse find it to be reasonable?

The key here is to *address one expectation at a time*. Often, what we find in our work with couples is that all expectations are clumped together and one grade is assigned. This is problematic. There is a reason you received a school report card that was divided into math, reading, science and physical education. You were graded on each individual class. Some of us did well in reading and writing but poorly in math and science.

Individual grades helped us focus and place more energy where it needed to be directed without being overwhelmed. For example, when I (Gary) was growing up, I invested a ton of energy in math, but I was still never very good at it. It is the primary reason why I am not an accountant, CFO or business manager today. After years of struggling with my grades in math, countless attempts by tutors to help me and doing extra homework, I still was not an "A" student in math. Thankfully, I had parents who understood this, and they encouraged me to direct my energies into other areas.

Bottom line: Your expectations about marriage should not be lumped together; each needs its own individual category on your report card. Address expectations one at a time with your mate.

A recent cartoon shows a fourth-grade boy standing toe-to-toe and nose-to-nose with his teacher. Behind them looms a blackboard covered with math problems the boy hasn't finished. With rare perception, the boy says, "I'm not an underachiever, you're an overexpecter!"

We do not want you to be an underachiever or an overexpecter in your marriage. As you address each expectation separately, you will be able to strike a balance between unreasonable expectations and unhealthy reality.

2. Work on What You Can Change

Guess what you can change? You! You can change 100 percent of you and your expectations, but you cannot change all of your reality on your own. You can start by answering the first question: *Do I need to change or adjust my expectations?* This is the first step as you address each individual expectation.

Which of your expectations are reasonable or unreasonable? Which are based on biblical truth or not? In the upcoming chapters, we will walk through the different kinds of expectations men and women bring to marriage and show which expectations are biblical precepts or principles. Use the biblical precepts to help you filter through your individual expectations and adjust them as needed.

Remember, you are responsible for your expectations in the relationship. Recognizing how you need to change is the first step in bridging the gap between unreasonable expectations and unhealthy reality.

3. Release What You Cannot Change

Resolve to no longer force your mate to meet your expectations. You need to ask yourself: *Are my expectations fair and reasonable?*

You may have more unfair and unreasonable expectations than you realized. Now here's a little secret: Letting your mate off the hook will change the atmosphere of your marriage and home. Not only will you walk lighter, but so will your spouse.

What expectations do you need to release? Here are some examples from the chapter 1 assessment:

Long walks on the beach. We will walk for no other purpose but connecting. Just me and my spouse with the sand between our toes, pants rolled up and the tide coming in.
In-law visits once or twice a year. Mom and Dad will be able to set healthy boundaries without us needing to tell them. Visits will be minimal to help us "leave and cleave."

Nice house. We'll have a white picket fence, furniture, and backyard garden, or down-town loft. Maybe not necessarily our first home, but our home a few years down the road.
Romantic vacations. Cruises, beach houses or remote cabins in the Rockies. The honey-moon experience will happen at least once a year.
Home-cooked meals. My spouse will have the table set, dinner on the stove and even, at times, candles lit. Dinner out or ordered in will be infrequent. Meals at home, like momma use to make, will suffice.
Sex every day. Regular sex will solve any lust problems.
Sex all night. We will make love until the sun comes up. Multiple orgasms will be expe-rienced often.
One-income family. My spouse will make plenty of money to cover our expenses, so I can stay home with the kids.

We want to encourage you to reassess your expectations from chapter 1. Which expectations can and should you release?

4. Align Your Expectations with Reality

The goal is that you and your spouse will be able to sit down together and create new, realistic and biblical expectations for the future.

When I (Ted) became a father, my expectations were not aligned with my reality. For the first six months of parenthood, Amy and I were strained out with balancing marriage, childcare, career and sleep.

Most couples enjoy the idea of parenting. We prepare ourselves by reading books, taking classes and visiting the doctor at each stage of the pregnancy. Fun, sleek vehicles are traded in for more practical ones. Furniture is rearranged. Priorities change. For all the joy new parents experience, there is one thing we never prepare for: The Vacuum of Intimacy. When the pace of parenting destroys intimacy, the marriage is at risk.

I made a huge mistake early on. With two small kids at home, I took my wife for granted and let her get worn down. We started living like the butler and the maid. We became bondservants to our children. Our solution was simple: endure the childhood years like a military officer leading a small platoon. Then, in our later years, we planned to reconnect and enjoy life once again. Bad idea!

To top that off, I still had the expectations of spending a lot of time with friends and enjoying my hobbies. I kept pursuing life and work after Corynn was born. Amy and I were steadily disconnecting until the night we had a "Come to Jesus" meeting.

I'll never forget Amy sitting on the end of our bed in tears about the state of our family. She was growing cold and frustrated toward me. And it was totally understandable. I was acting like a fool. In our meeting that night, Amy reminded me of a story from a year earlier.

During the early years of church planting, we grew very close to our small group. We spent time each week with a number of young couples who shared our season of life. Some had children; some did not.

When we announced to our group that we were expecting, I said something that made sense to me but had no idea how bad it would hurt Amy. The result and fallout from those ill-chosen words would change our marriage forever. More importantly, it changed me forever.

I said, "Nothing is going to change once the baby is born." My words were not intended to hurt Amy, but it was my attempt to assure everyone that she and I would continue leading the church with all of our time and energy. This was an immature expectation, but I think I am not alone here. There must be a few hard-charging, goal-oriented men who feel the same way.

Amy heard my words in a completely different way, and it rocked her world. She heard, "We are still going to work long hours each week. We will still go out to dinner regularly with friends. We will put in long nights at church. Don't expect our lives or schedules to be any different." Nothing could have been further from the reality that would soon engulf our lives.

In our marriage conferences around the country, we teach that communication is more about what the other person is hearing and understanding, not what you are saying. Feelings are more important than words. A woman's intuition when it comes to the heart is like Superman's X-ray vision. Amy saw my heart when I spoke the words "Nothing will change." She knew I was not prepared for reality. I had making a baby all figured out. That part was fun. And the classes prepared me for the labor and delivery. However, I was not ready to be a dad. It would take me years to figure it all out. *Balancing marriage, career and parenting would prove to be the greatest challenge of my life.* While I still struggle each and every day with balance, I have experienced major breakthroughs.

That night, Amy shared with me, "Ted, I hope you know things *are* going to change. The baby will need naps, regular feedings and a schedule." Her beautiful eyes grabbed my attention and I could feel her heart as she gently said, "Everything is going to change."

That night was a turning point. I aligned my wrong expectations with reality.

It Isn't Easy, but It Is Worth It

In the midst of addressing the gap between our expectations and present reality, the Serenity Prayer by Reinhold Niebuhr reminds us that we do not need to be in control of everything around us, including people, places and things:

> *God, grant me the serenity*
> *to accept the things I cannot change;*

courage to change the things I can;
and wisdom to know the difference.
Living one day at a time;
Enjoying one moment at a time;
Accepting hardships as the pathway to peace;
Taking, as He did, this sinful world
as it is, not as I would have it;
Trusting that He will make all things right
if I surrender to His Will;
That I may be reasonably happy in this life
and supremely happy with Him
Forever in the next.
Amen.

On your wedding day, you often have a fairy tale world in your mind, a happily-ever-after story you will be a part of, with no problems, disagreements or concerns. The key to resolving the pain when these expectations are not met is to not adjust the behavior of your mate but rather take personal responsibility for your own expectations and, along with your mate, bring your expectations into reality and harmony with your mate's expectations. Both of you will discover that when you love each other and strive to become a "married team," you will both adjust your expectations to be in sync with reality and you will experience greater commitment to each other.

It's the gap between what you expect and what you actually experience that drains your energy. To reduce the stress, start making a list of all of your recalled expectations and start figuring out how to reduce the "gap" between those expectations and reality. (I show how to do that in my book *Your Relationship with God*.) When your experience is close to what you anticipated, you are stronger and more content, and that contentment bolsters your ability to keep on loving. But unless you talk about those things and bring your expectations to the surface, your mate may not know your desires, and you may find yourself facing an energy-sapping gap between your desires and your reality.

As you begin to understand God's expectation for you and your marriage, His Spirit will reveal areas that require change and convict you of the need to change. Remember, you cannot change your spouse. But God gives you the power to change yourself. You can trust and believe that God works in the lives of others to grow and change them in ways that you cannot.

After you've realigned your expectations, you need to look for ways to live out the changes you have made. Here are three principles to help you maintain healthy expectations of your marriage relationship.

Principle 1: Recharge Your Life Battery on a Regular Basis

I (Gary) bought a used motor home several months ago. My wife and I had a great conversation the week before I bought it. We enjoyed dreaming together about how we'd use the motor home to spend more time with our family. We'd travel in it with our grandchildren. We'd go on weekend getaways to Lake Taneycomo or Table Rock Lake. We would buy a little tiny piece of land, park it there, walk down to the water and swim with our grandchildren. We could let the kids use it. By the end of our conversations, I was convinced that we were both ready to begin shopping for a motor home.

While visiting Springfield, Missouri, I had some free time. I drove by a motor home dealership. My eyes were drawn to a used motor home with a brand-new engine. I noticed that it was a 1991 motor home but I quickly rationalized that with a new engine the year didn't really matter.

The salesman opened up the door and let me walk through. I loved it. It had been refurbished on the inside. I thought, *Wow, this is it!* The salesman negotiated an amazingly low price, and I was sold. I could picture the smile on Norma's face when I pulled this big baby into the driveway. She'd be thrilled. She'd run into my arms and I'd show her my amazing purchase. Our dreams were going to become reality.

I handed the salesman a check, and after signing a few documents I sat behind the wheel. It felt good to drive our new traveling home out of the parking lot. But within a few miles I had my first suspicions that something wasn't right. The engine had a slight, irregular rumble.

Norma's response when I pulled in the driveway was more horrified than happy. *What had I done?!* She wanted to know what possessed me to buy a used motor home on a whim. I backpedaled.

"I'm sorry," I said. "I thought you'd like it. I think there's a lemon law that allows us to take it back within three days. Besides, we just talked about this. You dreamed with me how we would take our grandkids and stay by the lake overnight. You told me how much fun it will be to drive to some remote places here in Missouri that don't even have a motel but do have camping spots to rent. But you said . . ."

I took the motor home back to the dealership the next morning. The salesman informed me that the lemon law didn't apply in Missouri.

What was I going to do?

I figured I would just sell it and try to get the same, if not close, to the price I paid for it.

In the meantime, I asked my son Michael, "Do you want a used motor home to get to Houston for your next seminar?"

"That would be great, Dad!" he replied.

I knew that if the trip went well, he'd want to buy the rig. The only problem with my plan is that on the way to Texas, the motor home broke down. A tiny wire on the transmission split. With little time to find a mechanic, he had to rent a car, drive to Texas, speak, and then come back and get the motor home repaired. He barely made it home.

"Dad, I hate that thing!" he announced.

My plan was unraveling.

So I took it to the mechanic. He noted that the engine needed a simple repair. I paid the bill and began driving it around town again.

Our daughter, Kari, then asked to borrow the motor home. I excitedly agreed to loan it to her and her family. But within a few blocks of our home, the motor home broke down in the middle of a three-way intersection.

I had to call a tow truck. Once the motor home was fixed, I offered to loan it to Greg, my other son. He graciously declined.

"You're not going to use it?" I challenged.

"No one wants to use it, Dad," he said. "My wife doesn't want to be in it. My kids don't want to be in it. No one has had a good experience with it."

Greg's honestly finally compelled me to get rid of the motor home. I fixed it up and sold it for far less than I paid for it.

During the whole time, my stomach felt sick. I began putting myself down in my mind, belittling myself for my foolish decision. I started running myself down with discouragement and hopelessness. That kind of thinking made me, Norma and the rest of my family miserable. Finally, I had to let it go. I had to turn over my mistake and foolishness to God and ask Him to expose me to His lovingkindness and grace.

Some of the highest expectations we hold are for ourselves. I know that when I don't meet my own expectations, there's always a temptation to belittle myself with negative self-talk. But what I'm finding is that I need to take a different approach. I've begun recognizing those moments for what they are: an opportunity to celebrate my weaknesses. Scripture reminds us, "My grace is sufficient for you, for my power is made perfect in weakness" (2 Cor. 12:9). Our weaknesses are an opportunity for God to be glorified. In fact, God's strength is made perfect when I am weak. When I realize this, then I can have a healthier approach to my short-comings. And Norma can tell you that I become a whole lot more pleasant to be around!

Stress brings out the worst in all of us! It's no surprise that stress comes from our unfulfilled expectations. One of my biggest stress buttons is related to time. I have a tendency to place time limits on everything—my schedule, my projects, my work. Slowly, I'm learning to lift self-imposed time limits; and whenever I do, my stress level diminishes rapidly. Whenever I give more time to myself to get stuff done, I enjoy the process a whole lot more.

A few years ago, I made a list of expectations in my life. I filled up four-and-a-half pages. Then I took those pages of expectations and placed them at the feet of Jesus. I told God that in spite of all my other ideas, all I really wanted was Him, His living and powerful words and the Holy Spirit to fill my life. When God's Spirit and His words are alive inside of me, I have access to unlimited power, unlimited love, unlimited fulfillment and unlimited life. What more could I truly expect or need?

Whenever I place my expectations at the feet of Jesus, I can let go of the little things and focus on Him instead. I still have huge expectations, but now they are all on "things above, not on earthly things" (Col. 3:2). I have loved seeing God's faithfulness at work within me as I rest in Him and His words through the power of His Spirit. This is not a "pipe dream" expectation; it has become reality for me. He's my life, and about 100 of His most important Bible verses have become branded upon my heart through memorizing them and meditating on them several times a day. Nothing has changed me more and given me more fulfillment than meditating on His words and resting in Him daily for all the life I'll ever need.

Principle 2: Choose to Enjoy Life Even When Expectations Go Unmet

Let's take a look once more at those expectations from chapter 1 to discern between the usual expectations and those guided by precepts or principles from Scripture. My dad's favorite saying while I (Ted) was growing up was, "We're not pessimists, we're realists." In other words, we just see life as it is and think nothing more of it.

Would you consider yourself to be an optimist? How about a pessimist? Or maybe you fall into the category of realist. Most of us will come to a point in life when we realize life is painful and disappointing. We recognize that not all of our dreams are going to come true. But even though not all the expectations we carried into marriage will be realized, we can still enjoy life. We can enjoy our marriage and dream new dreams.

Some disappointment in life is inevitable. Everyone experiences the pain of unmet expectations on some level. How much pain have you experienced in your life? Solomon knew something about this kind of pain:

> The words of the Teacher, son of David, king in Jerusalem: "Meaningless! Meaningless!" says the Teacher. "Utterly meaningless! Everything is meaningless." What does man gain from all his labor at which he toils under the sun? Generations come and generations go, but the earth remains forever. The sun rises and the sun sets, and hurries back to where it rises. The wind blows to the south and turns to the north; round and round it goes, ever turning on its course. All streams flow into the sea, yet the sea is never full. To the place the streams come from, there they return again (Eccles. 1:1-7).

Look again at that sentence from the Scripture passage you just read: "Generations come and generations go, but the earth remains forever."

You and I are here on earth for only a short period of time. At best, we can manage pain, but we can't remove it.

Mankind has always looked for ways to get around the fact that life is hard. We try different pursuits. Some people continually look for just the right relationship and move on to a new relationship whenever they are disappointed or hurt.

If you're trying to fill your life by skipping from relationship to relationship in order to take care of the problem of disappointed expectations, then you, too, know that it doesn't solve the core problem . . . that life is hard. Solomon had hundreds of wives and hundreds of concubines. (What in the world was he thinking?!) All those relationships still didn't satisfy him.

Some people try to fill their life with money. Some of the most miserable individuals I've ever met are people who have a lot of money. Money does not fix the problems of life. Getting more stuff doesn't fix the problem of life. Both the poor and the rich get cancer.

Solomon was the king of Jerusalem. He had the position, prestige and money and all the stuff a person could want, and you know what he said about it? He gets to the end and realizes that the pursuit of all that stuff is, "Meaningless! Meaningless! Utterly meaningless!"

So where do we find meaning? Where do we find purpose? Solomon gives us illustrations from nature. Nature is going to keep going. This world is going to keep going. Life is going to keep going . . . while you are here and after you die. There is nothing on this earth that can give us our true purpose, nothing that earth or this life has to offer. There has to be something more than what we have already tried.

Walk on any college campus and you'll find building after building with names above the door. You don't have a clue about who that person was or what they did to earn a spot on the sign. At one time, they were popular. At one time they were known.

Most banks have a plaque with someone's name on it, stating when the building was constructed and when it was dedicated. I have never walked into a bank to hear someone say, "Wow! So-and-so was here when this building was dedicated in 1952!" Do you know why? We really don't care. Can't you just hear Solomon say, "What we do today will be forgotten tomorrow. All things are wearisome more than one can say."

So where do we find ultimate fulfillment? If it is not in our name, our money, relationships or thrills, where does it reside?

Principle 3: Never Lose Sight of the Source of Life

Your relationship with Christ is the source of your best possible life. You can expect the best when He is your source of fulfillment. "Keep your lives free from the love of money and be content with what you have, because God has said, 'Never will I leave you; never will I forsake you'" (Heb. 13:5).

Our moods change. Our income fluctuates. Our name gets slandered. If we hold on to those things rather than the true source, we will be disappointed and let down. But since God is faithful, He will fill your life with all the fullness of Himself . . . you can count on it! When He says that if you seek Him and His righteousness, and if you will humble yourself (admit that you are helpless spiritually), He will never disappoint you; He will fill your life to overflowing with unimaginable miracles.

Recently, our friends in the Christian rock/contemporary music band Rush of Fools were nominated for four Dove Awards. We all expected great things for them. On the night the awards were presented, I (Ted) sent a text message to Kevin Huguley, the leader of the band. It simply read, "How is your night going?" His text back read, "We did not receive a thing. God is sovereign." I then told him the story about when I won the American Legion School Award at my high school graduation in 1992. Not one word has been spoken since that day about that reward.

When I (Gary) won two academy-type awards in both the world and the Church, no one ever asked to see those awards in my office. I don't even think about them. Oh, how quickly we forget! When we attempt to be the source of our fulfillment, we must learn to laugh and lighten up. We really have only one source. Life is all about our relationship with God and with each other. Nothing matters more than His love given to us so that we can love Him more and love each other. No amount of money, things or success will ever match our loving relationship with our Creator and with others.

When Lloyd C. Douglas, author of *The Robe* and other novels, was a university student, he lived at a boarding house. Downstairs on the first floor was an elderly retired music teacher. He was infirm and unable to leave the apartment. Douglas said that every morning they had a ritual they would go through together. Douglas would come down the steps, open the old man's door and ask, "Well, what's the good news?" The old man would pick up his tuning fork, tap it on the side of his wheelchair and say, "That's middle C! It was middle C yesterday; it will be middle C tomorrow; it will be middle C a thousand years from now. The tenor upstairs sings flat, the piano across the hall is out of tune, but, my friend, that is middle C!"[1]

The old man had discovered one thing upon which he could depend, one constant reality in his life, one still point in a turning world. The one still point in a turning world, the one absolute of which there is no shadow of turning, is Jesus Christ (see Jas. 1:17).

What have you found to be constant in your life? Your mate will change, for better or worse. You will change. Your finances will change. Your health will change. But Christ never changes.

I start every morning, and continue throughout the day, by focusing on the reality of Christ. That doesn't mean I sit in an ivory tower. I am fully engaged in life and my relationships with others. But because

I return my focus to Christ as frequently as possible, I have never been more full of peace, joy, love and gratitude; and I have never felt more overflowing with life. Here is a look at how I meditate on the Lord and His Word:

1. I wake up every morning and admit that I am helpless spiritually and thank Him for giving me more of His Kingdom of love and power. (See Matt. 5:3; Jas. 4:6; Matt. 22:37.)

2. I thank God for sending His only Son to save me and give me an overflowing, powerful and loving life through Him. (See Rom. 10:9-10; Eph. 2:8-9.) He freely gives me His grace (love and power) even though I am not worthy.

3. I thank Jesus for sending me His Holy Spirit to remind me of what He told us when He was alive on earth, and the Holy Spirit empowers me to live and act like Him. (See Acts 1:8.)

4. I thank Him for all disappointments, trials and any difficulty I might face today or that I'm now facing. (See Rom. 5:3-5; 2 Cor. 12:9-10; 1 Thess. 5:16-18; Rom. 8:28.)

5. I thank God that He gives me His love and power to fulfill man's highest job: loving and serving others in the same way that I love myself. (See Matt. 22:39; Gal. 5:13-14.)

Expecting the best starts with a solid foundation in Christ. What is your life grounded in?

In the next chapter, we will look at the power of practicing outrageous love in marriage. You will learn three specific ways you can increase the fragrance of love in your marriage and get a list of more than 30 ideas of how you can display random acts of kindness to your spouse.

FROM GARYSMALLEY.COM

This question was sent to our website by a woman who is struggling with her weight and how it is impacting her relationship with her husband.

Q: *My husband (36) and I (40) have been married for six years and are both strongly involved in our church. During our marriage, I have struggled with gaining weight. My husband has become very distant and has come straight out and told me, "You need to lose weight! I don't like it!" I do my best to eat healthy and stay away from junk food 95 percent of the time. I know I haven't exercised enough, but I started hitting the gym daily a couple of weeks ago. My husband sees that I am trying but is still distant. He constantly mentions the young, pretty women he works with and is not acting toward me the way he used to. My self-esteem is gone. I pray, pray, pray. What else should I do? He promises me there is no one else. I feel sad and confused!*

A: Let me start by saying that you and your weight are not the core issue here. Getting healthy and taking care of your body are both good things. But from what you have described, your health is not your primary concern.

When we say that the issue is not the issue, we mean that there is an emotion hidden behind the issue. For instance,

- Is your husband *worried* for your health and quality of life?
- Is he *embarrassed* to be seen with you?
- Is he *uncomfortable* making love to you?
- Is he *disconnected* because he is interested in other women?

Your weight is not the real issue. The reality is that you could lose the weight and wear a size 2 or 4 dress and he might still be uninterested in you, especially if he is emotionally involved with other women. Your husband needs to deal with his own issues and his heart. All I can do is help you with your heart. Do not allow your husband's heart to keep you from growing in the Lord. As a child of God, you are loved. His love is not based on the numbers on your bathroom scale.

You and I have the same choice to make—and our choice will largely determine whether we enjoy deep, satisfying relationships or fragile, disappointing ones. I can't stress enough how crucial it is that each one of us takes personal responsibility for how we think and respond within our relationships.

By nature, most of us want to blame those who upset us. We work hard to try to get them to change how they treat us. We attempt in many unhealthy ways to manipulate them. In the end, we wind up feeling hurt, abused, estranged and lonely—and one more relationship takes a tragic turn for the worse.

To take personal responsibility means that you refuse to focus on what your husband has done or said. You cannot change your husband's approach to your weight issue any more than he can change your weight.

Working with your pastor, small-group leader or a professional counselor will help you work through these issues. Ask God to help you ignore the voices in your head that tell you falsehoods about yourself, and know today that you are unconditionally loved by God!

CHAPTER 7

EXTRAVAGANT LOVE

We have talked a lot about the expectations we bring to marriage and how those expectations seldom line up with the reality of our experience. If you were to go back to the list from chapter 1, I wonder how many of those expectations were based on your receiving something rather than giving something in your marriage? If John F. Kennedy were wording the ruling principle in marriage, it would sound something like: "Ask not what your spouse can do for you, but what you can do for your spouse."

The healthiest list of expectations you can have for yourself is based on what you give to your spouse. So you need to start a new list of expectations based on what you expect to give to your mate.

I received a new debit card from my bank a few weeks ago. I slipped it into my wallet. Later that day, I pulled it out and handed it to a clerk. The transaction was denied. Why? Because I had to activate the card before I could use it. I think that's a great word picture for my own faith journey. All too often, God desires to give me something, but I don't get it because I don't choose to cry out to God for His power and strength. Instead, I just think that whatever I need will be available whenever I need it. I become self-reliant instead of God-reliant.

All good things come from above. God is the source of our strength, hope and growth. God is also the source of love, because He is love (see 1 John 4:16). Now, of all the things God gives us, love is considered the greatest, and those who claim to be followers of Jesus Christ are supposed to be marked by this love. We are called to love unconditionally—in marriage and in other relationships.

One of our greatest opportunities is to love unconditionally when we find ourselves facing unmet expectations. But even better news for humans is that we don't have to use our own "puny" human love. We are commanded to love God with all of our heart, soul, mind and strength; but we don't have to use human love. The second greatest commandment, the commandment that covers all other commandments, is to love our neighbor just like we love ourselves; but we don't have to use our measly love! We get to use God's love, freely given to anyone who humbles himself before Him. When we admit that we are "poor in God's Spirit," God gives us His very kingdom of heaven (see Matt. 5:3): He gives us His power and love. That's what Scripture means by telling us that God only gives His grace (undeserved and freely given power and love from God) to the humble (see Jas. 4:6). The people who are humble are those who recognize and admit that they are bankrupt of God's love, helpless on their own to muster up God's love, or shipwrecked of God's love.

Grace to the humble is one of the most important truths in the entire Bible. When we realize that God wants to give us His overflowing and abundant love, all we have to do is recognize the obvious: humans can't love like God loves; therefore, we need His love in us to carry out His most important will—to love Him with all that we have and love others with the same love with which we wish to be loved! Is that not amazing? So, from now on in this book, when we mention how powerful love is for your relationships with both God and people, we want you to be aware that we are not talking about human love. We are talking about God giving you His love in abundant measure.

When you are tempted to feel hurt or disappointed, choose instead to live out of the love that God gives you; it has a transforming power that people can't help but notice. It is extravagant, outrageous love. It is the kind of love that you are to infuse in your marriage. Let's first look at examples of extravagant love from the Bible, then we'll give you three insights on how to infuse your marriage with the kind of love God designed marriage to contain.

Outrageous Love

Did you know that your marriage is actually a testimony to the world about God? John 13:35 says, "Your love for one another will prove to the world that you are my disciples" (*NLT*). Notice that there aren't any exceptions to the phrase "one another." That means that your love for your spouse proves to the world that you are a disciple of Jesus. In other words, people are watching you and how you live your life.

One of the most memorable accounts of love found in the gospels is in John 12. We read that six days before Passover, Jesus arrived in Bethany and eventually went to the home of Lazarus. Now Jesus had raised Lazarus from the dead, and a dinner had been prepared in Jesus' honor.

I want you to imagine the conversation around the table. Someone turns to Lazarus and asks, "So, how's your week gone?" "Well, I died on Tuesday and kind of laid around the grave for a few days. Then Jesus raised me over the weekend. Could you pass the salt, please?" All the while, his sister Martha is serving food.

In the midst of this setting, sister Mary takes an expensive perfume made from essence of nard, which is a fragrance that comes from the root of a plant grown in northern India. It's not the kind of product you just have a lot of laying around the home. She opens the bottle, releasing the rich fragrance. Then she anoints Jesus' feet with it and wipes his feet with her hair.

If you've ever been around an unrestrained gesture of love, you know that it feels a little awkward. To make matters worse, what Mary is doing is taboo. In that culture, the only person for whom a woman would let down her hair was her husband.

In the Song of Solomon, one of my favorite books of the Bible, the woman goes into the bridal chamber and begins to undress (see Song of Solomon 4). In the most intimate of acts, sexual intercourse with her husband, the first thing the bride does is take the pin out of her hair. Her beautiful locks fall down and her king compares her hair to a flock of goats descending from Gilead. Now that may seem like a strange comment, but her husband had spent time on the rocky mountain. He had watched flocks of goats go down its slopes. He remembered that beautiful scene as his wife let her hair down and it flowed over her shoulders.

Though the encounter of Mary and Jesus is not one of sexual intimacy, it's still one of intimacy. And that creates awkwardness when you're breaking through cultural taboos and expressing abounding love.

Judas Iscariot spoke up. He challenged this act of love, noting that it would have been better to sell the perfume and give the money to the poor. But Jesus defends Mary's act of love.

What character in this story—Mary or Judas—do you most look like when it comes to expressing love in your marriage? Do you show unrestrained love toward your mate, or are you constantly calculating the cost?

All too often I hear comments from couples like these:

"My husband is no longer responding to me."
"We have slipped into monotony in our marriage."
"There's no desire to serve each other anymore."
"Our love has grown cold."

These comments flow from a marriage in which the acts of God's love no longer exist. The routine of life has created a vacuum where intimacy should be. Routine has been interpreted as boredom, frustration and an attitude of fatigue toward the relationship. That makes sense, because human love fades, but God's love increases in power and affection.

I (Gary) have noticed over the past four years how my love and affection for Norma has increased dramatically. I so want to please her, like never before. We've been in the process of building a new house, and I can't help but notice how much I don't hassle her at all anymore. She is getting a chance, in her sixth decade, to finally "nest" in her home and buy things that truly reflect who she is. I've always interfered to some degree in making sure that many of the things in our house reflected me; but now I can't help my new desire to see that she finally gets what I should have been willing to give her during all the 43 years of our marriage. But I'm not forcing myself to have any of my new attitudes or feelings to please her. I can tell that my new love and power is coming from outside of me and it is changing me daily.

Ways to Seek God's Love

I hope you are now convinced that it's essential to look for ways to seek God's love every day, all day long. That's the only way you can lavish your spouse with God's love. Do you need to change the fragrance of your marriage? Here are three ways to do that:

1. Catch Yourself Doing the *Unexpected*

Like Mary, each of us has the opportunity to do the unexpected for our spouse. We can surprise our spouse and even take his/her breath away with our acts of kindness, generosity and love.

All too often, the busyness of life keeps us from truly loving on our spouse in unexpected ways. Yet, if we slow down and begin paying attention, most of us will discover countless opportunities right in front of us. Like Mary, we may have spur-of-the-moment opportunities to lavish our spouse with love.

Sometimes doing the unexpected means simply breaking the routine.

When I (Ted) leave home in the morning, it is usually during extreme chaos. Kissing Amy is a priority, but not always easy. She is often distracted. But a few weeks ago we had a major breakthrough that we negotiated by doing the unexpected.

I said to her, "When I leave in the morning, you are often distracted, but I try not to take it personally. I don't need a grand parade when I leave, but the feeling of 'I will miss you' would be nice. What can I do to make the morning exit flow better?" My wife does not usually get very vocal with her opinions, but when she does it comes in the form of a bulleted list.

"I'm glad you asked," she said. "There are several things you could do around here before you head out the door. They're not great big things, but they are little, simple gestures that show you care. Would you like me to share some?"

"Sure," I said. What else was I going to say? So, I braced myself.

"If you would put the dishes in the sink after breakfast, help get the family picked up or see if the kids need anything before you go, that would help a lot," Amy said.

Then it hit me. My exit in the morning was all about me: making sure my bag was packed; finding my keys; getting my wallet and pouring my to-go cup of coffee. What Amy was looking for was not absolutely critical, but her suggestions communicated, "It is not just about you, Ted!" Amy gets three people ready every morning, five out of seven days a week, while I worry about one person, me. For me to even ask Amy what I can do to help her in the morning is evidence that God is giving me the desire and the ability.

Saying to Amy "Is there anything I can do for you before I leave" was like my hearing from her, "Ted, you need to call up some buddies and go fishing." It changed everything. Why? It was so unexpected. You want to go one step further with me? When I find something to do without even asking... *Whoa!* She is now ready for sex! I no longer use the word "foreplay" in our home. We replaced it with choreplay, listeningplay, understandingplay, spendingtimeplay or... you get the point!

Warning: Breaking routine, identifying and doing something that needs to be done or even asking how you can help may require picking your spouse up off the floor.

2. Catch Yourself Doing the *Unaffordable*

You've probably seen the TV show *Extreme Home Makeover*. I'm a big fan of that show. I loved the first season and was blown away by the love shown in reality. Now that we are a few seasons in, I caught myself just last week looking over at Amy while we were watching a show we had recorded, and I said, "This family didn't even get a pool! They get a house and no pool?! The last couple got a $200,000 check, and these people didn't get a car or a check; the show must have a smaller budget!"

The thing I love about *Extreme Home Makeover* isn't their ability to build a home in seven days or Ty Pennington yelling, "Move . . . that . . . bus!" For me, it's the outrageous generosity that families experience and the tender care and concern the building team shows as they get to know each person in a family before they plan and build the home. The team manages to build something that goes beyond every family member's expectations. It's so over the top that we're often left in awe of the display of relational and physical generosity.

Doing the unaffordable does not mean draining your bank account. But it does mean allocating dollars toward another's needs and desires rather than your own. Doesn't God operate that way? He sent His Son to live, teach us His eternal wisdom, suffer and die; then He used His eternal power to defeat death once and for all. That's over-the-top love!

Unfortunately, there is evidence every day in the news of man's need for this "over the top love." Mankind is so desperate for God's love because of its evil tendencies, and I (Gary) experienced this in a very personal way a few years ago. On October 6, 2004, at 4:20 A.M., Norma's greatest fear in life materialized. I could have avoided this entire situation for her if only I had taken the time to do a honey-do list of fixing the garage door lock when she asked for it a few months earlier.

I was out of town. Norma was alone. It all started with the sound of breaking glass. She jumped out of bed and immediately checked to see if the bedroom door was locked. It was. Soon she heard more noises; first like the sound of someone screaming; then moments later, something like the sound of an eerie chant. Norma was terrified.

In the early morning hours, a man had broken into our home. As we discovered later, he had overdosed on methamphetamines and was having a drug-induced psychotic episode. (A year later, he was sent to a mental institution for criminals.)

This man had jumped off his 16-foot balcony and shattered his ankle. He limped across the street, dragging his foot behind him and crashed through our garage window, falling hard on the glass and debris and cutting himself severely. But he felt no pain because of the methamphetamines. Bleeding profusely, he broke through the garage door and entered our home. He was convinced that demons were out to kill him as he careened through our house, knocking over furniture and wrecking our decor. From where Norma hid, the noise seemed deafening. She was sure he would find her; it was simply a matter of time.

As fear tightened its grip on her, she instinctively did the exact thing that TV talk show hosts had taught her. She ran into the bathroom and locked herself in the toilet area. The intruder would have to break through three heavy doors to get to her. Norma then dialed 911. (I am so thankful we followed through on installing a phone in our bathroom!) Within three minutes a police officer had arrived, but he could not enter our home because he wasn't sure how many people were inside. He needed backup. So he waited in our driveway for additional officers to show up.

Meanwhile, Norma endured 20 minutes of this man screaming, chanting and destroying our stuff—the longest 20 minutes of her life. Several times the screams were so close that she was terrified he was about to burst through the door into our bedroom. "He's coming in, he's coming in," she cried to the 911 operator. The operator reassured Norma that the police were ready to burst in if he actually entered the bedroom. Ultimately, the deranged man barricaded himself against his demons inside the closet of a second-floor bedroom—the room right above Norma.

When the police finally apprehended the man, they found blood on the door handle of our bedroom. He had ventured all the way to our bedroom door, but for some reason he had stopped. Norma believes that God's angels stood there with their hands outstretched, telling him he could go no farther.

On that October night, Norma's worst fears were realized. She thought she was secure in our home because we had a state-of-the-art home security system. The only problem was that the system had not been activated that night.

That was more than four years ago, and Norma still is very uneasy when I am out of town. For the longest time after that terrible event, Norma begged me to up the security around our home. This request for heightened security included floodlights to cover every inch of our yard, lights on all four corners of the house and window shades in the bedroom. In proportion to our household budget, this was not a lot of money. We figured out that the motion sensor floodlights on the four corners of the house would cover pretty much the entire house.

At first I dragged my feet on this project. It was during a time of ministry when I was gone more than I was home; and when I was home, I was catching up on books and projects. But driven by God's love within me, I was motivated to act on her behalf. It was easy to call in the electricians and other repairmen to add whatever Norma needed to feel more secure.

On a side note, I have watched Norma seek more of God's love and power as a result of this break-in. She is beginning to write her own book about how God gives us more of His grace through difficult situations. I hear her singing every day, "This is the day that the Lord has made . . . I will rejoice and be glad in it." She has learned to be much more grateful for everything in life, including the crud that hits all of us from time to time. With every difficulty, God gives more and more of His patience, godly character and hope to those who express thanks. And hope is never disappointed, because God pours into the grateful more of His love through His Holy Spirit.

Nothing screams "I Love You" more than when you carve out extravagant time for your spouse. Enthusiasm to serve your spouse happens when God is pushing you along with His power and love. His grace is at work within us even though we don't deserve it, and that's what makes it His love. We don't have to repay Him or earn it in any way. Now isn't that a deal and a half?

3. Catch Yourself Doing Something *Now*

One of the things I love about the story of Mary and the perfume she poured on Jesus' feet is Jesus' response to her outrageous act of generosity. In Mark 14:6-8, Jesus defends her, saying, "Leave her alone. Why criticize her for doing such a good thing to me? You will always have the poor among you, and you can help them whenever you want to. But you will not always have me. She has done what she could and has anointed my body for burial ahead of time" (*NLT*).

Notice that Jesus describes Mary anointing His body "ahead of time." I believe those words embody what the Do It Now principle is all about. It means not waiting to do what you can do. Mary gave what she had and what she could give in the moment. The result was an extravagant, extreme, unrestrained gesture of love. Don't wait to do what is right and needed now.

Procrastination is the enemy of intimacy. Its message says, "You are not important enough to me to drop everything I am doing to do something for you." That unfinished project is not so much about the date of completion as it is about the value you place on the relationship you have with the one who asked you to do it.

Another hard lesson learned early in our marriage (Ted's) was how to handle errands. When Amy would call and say she needed something on the way home from work, I would respond with "Can it wait?" What Amy heard was "Can you wait?"

Recently, our youngest was sick with a pretty bad ear infection. We had taken him to the doctor and he was doing better, but the medicine was running out. Amy called me at work and asked if I could get his prescription filled. Instead of asking if it could wait until I was on the way home, I tried something different. Yes, it could probably wait, but that was not the point. Amy did not need to say a word. I knew a better response. So I asked, "Would you like me to bring it home at lunch?"

She responded with, "No, it can wait."

Immediacy ignites intimacy. It says, "You are important to me. Enough so that I will drop everything I am doing to serve you." It has only taken 12 years and hundreds of moronic episodes for me to figure out this lesson.

Don't wait until all your expectations are met to express extravagant love to your spouse. Instead, lavish your spouse with love today. You'll be amazed at the results! And do it even before God gives you His love, if you can, because after He infuses you with His type of love, you'll have that "want-to feeling" and it may even surprise you at times. I know some people who won't move out and love others until they feel it. You need to do what is right no matter how you feel.

Unexpected, Unaffordable, Immediate Acts of Love

1. Ask if your spouse needs assistance with anything before you leave the house.
2. Take initiative with a chore or two.
3. Grab his/her hand as you stroll across the parking lot.
4. Open a car door.
5. Pull back the chair to offer your wife a seat at dinner.
6. Hug and kiss your spouse before you leave, or when you get home.
7. Sell something on eBay that you've treasured but is collecting dust and give your wife the money for something she wants.
8. Organize, set up and run a garage sale to pay for your spouse's next season's clothes.
9. Use your airline miles to invite your mate on your next work trip.
10. Offer to take your mate's car, so she/he can get the newer one (even if yours was next to be traded in).
11. Stop off at the car wash for 30 minutes and get a complete detail for the family vehicle.
12. Call before you come home to see if anything is needed at the store.
13. Run a bath for your mate.
14. Offer a quickie to your husband.
15. Bring home one flower. Most guys think a dozen flowers are necessary to achieve the "wow" effect, when most times one flower is just as powerful.
16. Hire a maid service just once to clean the whole house from top to bottom.
17. Hire a yard service to mow and weed.
18. Hire someone to clean the outside windows.
19. Hire a handyman for those little household problems you have been promising to fix.
20. Take the kids out for the afternoon and give your spouse some R and R at home.

21. Do a chore that has been the other's responsibility for years.

22. Take your spouse's car to do Sunday errands or to church just so you can fill up the gas tank for the workweek ahead.

23. Give up lattes for one month and drink regular coffee. This could save you $50 to $100. Use that money to buy a round of golf or a spa treatment for your mate.

24. Plan a weekend getaway. Last-minute deals are available on all of the travel websites. Spontaneity merges the unexpected with the immediate.

25. Don't underestimate breaking out of the routine on date nights. Go beyond movies and restaurants. Visit a fish hatchery (very popular thing to do in Missouri), take a tour of a winery (if applicable in your area) or stroll through a museum.

26. Plan a date day, not just an evening. Rent a boat at a local marina. A two-hour drive ain't a bad thing. Pack a lunch or dinner and eat while trolling the shoreline.

27. Try a sport you have never tried before. Bowling, tennis, hiking or fishing are all reasonably priced activities.

28. Take a tour of open houses in your area. The model homes in new housing developments are fun to tour and are free. Plus it's a great way to get decorating ideas.

29. Rent your mate's favorite movie and make popcorn.

30. Drive your mate to a favorite place and ask him/her to share what would make this year a favorite year if _____ happened.

31. Make something by hand that your mate loves.

32. Discuss a disagreement with your mate and determine ahead of time that you'll stick with the discussion until you both love the solution you came up with together.

33. Fix something around the house that your mate has mentioned and let him/her discover it.

34. Ask your mate for date or activity ideas that you can use sometime in the future as a surprise.

Our ways are so different from God's ways; His are higher and better. If we understand this, we can decide to show care and concern before we start seeing God's love and power flowing through us. Remember, He only gives His grace to the humble. I love that, because my natural nature doesn't even come close to His ways, so I need His love and power every day to face loving others and dealing with adversity.

Now that we've given you a vision of how to unleash love in your relationship, it's time to look at the heart of a loving spouse. In the next chapter, we're going to examine some dicey issues, including how submission works in a marriage without reaction. Both men and women walk into a relationship with expectations of order and partnership. No matter the roles you've established in your marriage, you're going to discover 10 actions that honor your spouse.

FROM GARYSMALLEY.COM

This question was sent to our website by a husband who is questioning how to balance family and work.

Q: *My wife says I love going to work more than being with the family. She believes I live by the motto "Career first, family second." I am the primary provider. How do I balance work and family?*

A: Balancing all areas of life can be quite challenging! I have had similar conversations with my wife over the years.

I have taken the following steps in letting my wife and children know how important they are to me.

1. *Tell the members of your family how valuable they are to you every day.* That's so simple, so obvious. You would assume they

already know it. But don't assume! Like a lightbulb that doesn't light due to a break in the electric circuit, family members who are not told they are valuable may never shine bright. Until you complete the circuit with your words, the light of honor may never glow in their lives.

2. *Make an unconditional commitment to your spouse and children for life.* That's the kind of commitment that says, "You're important to me today and tomorrow, no matter what happens—no matter what the cost."

3. *Schedule special times with your family.* Communicating warm, loving approval by your presence and your words doesn't "just happen" naturally. This time should be scheduled and take place on a regular basis—preferably several times a week—because your family needs you and you need them.

4. *Communicate your availability to your family during both scheduled and unscheduled times.* Although every one of us leads a busy life, there will be times when we need to drop what we're doing and make ourselves available to our family. Being available communicates that you value them above whatever else you are doing and also allows you to take advantage of teachable moments.

I remember one day a number of years ago when everything came crashing down. It was a hectic time at the church, but I decided to go home and have lunch with Norma. I bounded enthusiastically into the kitchen and said, "Hey, what's for lunch?" When I tried to hug her, she bristled and wouldn't turn around.

"What's wrong?" I asked.

"Nothing you want to hear." She stood at the sink, cold and distant. It was like death standing there. I sat down, still wanting to eat, but nothing was prepared.

"Come on, tell me what's wrong?" I repeated two or three times.

Finally she responded. "What's the point? It never does any good. All you do is talk, but nothing ever changes. Everything else in your life is more important than I am. Your fishing, every kid you work with, everybody in church, every committee, the basketball team, the church building, even the television are all more important to you than I am. You come home and act like I don't even exist. You plop down and watch television or read the paper. Then you eat dinner, go off to some meeting or appointment and never even thank me."

I was utterly stunned. Yes, she had been reminding me about spending more time with her, but I had no idea it had come to this. Her words cut me to the core. I was being selfish. I had placed myself at the center of the universe and expected others to orbit around me. I had the "I want to be God" attitude. I wanted to be worshiped, admired, adored and blessed by others. That attitude drew my attention away from my home and to my church, where I found admirers ready to lay lavish accolades on me for my great work for the Kingdom.

"You are right," I said to Norma. "I admit it. I've made everything else in my life more important than you. Even fishing is more important to me than you. I am so ashamed. I promise right now that I will put you first in my life. You will be my number-one priority—above friends, fishing, counseling and even above the church. I may lose my job over it, but that's okay. I would rather lose my job than lose you. I beg you to forgive me. If you can't do it yet, I understand. Things didn't get in this shape overnight, and you may not believe I can really change."

That day I promised her that she would be my top priority over everything else on earth. But on my way back to work, a dark cloud descended on me as I realized that my life was now over. No more fishing, no more working late, no more golfing, no more weekends with friends—I was dead. I wanted to call her back when I returned to work and say, "I didn't really mean I would put you above *everything* else, just most things."

But by the power and grace of God, I did change. Every morning I got up looking for ways to serve my wife—to put her first over everything else. From that time on, I was always home at night. If someone called with a ministry request that would take me away, I said, "Sorry, I can't do that tonight. I'm with my wife and family." Norma heard those answers and, in time, they began to soften her attitude toward me.

It wasn't easy. I had to make a lot of tough decisions; but putting my family first was an investment I have never regretted. And it wasn't even a few months after making this important decision that Norma started pushing me to be more involved at work because she finally felt secure and knew I loved her more than my work.

CHAPTER 8

THE SERVANT

Sam is a blue-collar, hardworking guy. With the recent expansion of the highways in his area, he was working overtime every day. During these difficult economic times, the extra money helped the family's bottom line.

Lucy is Sam's understanding wife who works a full-time job as a sales associate. Her job is stressful. Both Sam and Lucy made the decision that she should avoid overtime for the sake of the family. Their love for each other made home life very much a team effort.

Lucy was constantly looking for ways to show her love and appreciation for Sam that were immediate, unexpected yet affordable. She made this effort from a spirit of personal responsibility. She clearly understood that she was all alone in seeking God's power to show love. She couldn't depend upon her parents, Sam or anyone else. As a living follower of Christ, she totally depended on His power and love to love others. Not a day goes by when she isn't figuratively on her knees, waiting for God to freshly infuse His love within her.

She and Sam are like so many other couples that marry with no expectation that they will need to work long hours to make ends meet, spend few hours together at home or stay stuck in jobs that are stressful. Even though that is reality for most couples, it's never anyone's marriage plan early on.

One of the acts of love Lucy expressed toward Sam was to pack his lunch every day. She packed great snacks as well as plenty to fill him up at the noon hour. Her goal was to make his fellow workers envious. One day, Lucy got the idea to write a simple note expressing her love and appreciation for all of his hard work. She slipped it between the granola bars and roast beef sandwich.

To her surprise that night as she was unpacking Sam's lunch cooler, she found a note that read: *"To the greatest wife in the world! Thank you for making my day and working so hard to serve me every day. I love you!"*

The old note in the lunch box or suitcase was not new, but the return message was! While Lucy and Sam have developed roles in their relationship, they do not take each other for granted. They still express their appreciation and love to each other. You cannot discuss expectations without discussing roles. We have roles at work, at church and at school. Yet when we discuss roles at home, the issue can get sticky and complicated.

Check out the article on pages 166-167 that we found in *Housekeeping Monthly* from 1955. I (Ted) have never laughed so hard in all my life!

In the upcoming chapter, we're going to look at the role every spouse should maintain in marriage, and it isn't related to job title. The role that every spouse should fulfill is the role of being a servant. We're going to unpack a rather sticky topic: the issue of submission and service. Then we're going to look at 10 Ways to Show Appreciation and Honor to Your Spouse.

Unhealthy Expectations Husbands Bring to Marriage:
- I make the decisions in this house.
- I earn more of the money, so I have the final decision on how it is spent.
- I can have sex on demand, whenever I want.
- She is the primary caregiver to the children.

Healthy Expectations Husbands Bring to Marriage:
- I get to be the lead servant, dying daily for my wife.
- We can discuss any and every issue together.

- Sexual intimacy is about serving, not getting.
- I have a biblical mandate to lead my family and raise my children in the admonition of the Lord and guide them to walk in His purposes.

Unhealthy Expectations Wives Bring to Marriage:
- He will never tell me what to do.
- I'll spend money however I please.
- Sex will be used as a weapon or reward.
- I will be a great mom and a lousy lover.

Healthy Expectations Wives Bring to Marriage:
- I get to honor and respect my husband in the home.
- I may oversee the budget, but we need to be united on the big-ticket items.
- Sexual intimacy is about serving, even if he needs more orgasms than me.
- I will find balance as a great lover and great mom.

So how do you handle the issue of expectations when it comes to marriage? The answer may be simpler than you think: *service*. The antidote for selfishness and the issue of unrealistic expectations can be cleared up with an attitude of serving one another. "Serve" is a simple word, but it is what God says is one of the most powerful words in all the Bible. All other commands follow this one (see Gal. 5:13-14). Servanthood summarizes all that Jesus stands for. When you catch yourself wanting to serve your mate, you know the desire comes from God.

What does serving your mate mean? For a man it means laying down his life for his wife—and choosing to love wholly. I (Gary) used to think

Housekeeping Monthly 13 May 1955

The good wife's guide

- Have dinner ready. Plan ahead, even the night before, to have a delicious meal ready, on time for his return. This is a way of letting him know that you have been thinking about him and are concerned about his needs. Most men are hungry when they come home and the prospect of a good meal (especially his favorite dish) is part of the warm welcome needed.

- Prepare yourself. Take 15 minutes to rest so you'll be refreshed when he arrives. Touch up your make-up, put a ribbon in your hair and be fresh-looking. He has just been with a lot of work-weary people.

- Be a little gay and a little more interesting for him. His boring day may need a lift and one of your duties is to provide it.

- Clear away the clutter. Make one last trip through the main part of the house just before your husband arrives.

Housekeeping Monthly 13 May 1955

- Gather up schoolbooks, toys, paper etc and then run a dustcloth over the tables.

- Over the cooler months of the year you should prepare and light a fire for him to unwind by. Your husband will feel he has reached a haven of rest and order, and it will give you a lift too. After all, catering for his comfort will provide you with immense personal satisfaction.

- Prepare the children. Take a few minutes to wash the children's hands and faces (if they are small), comb their hair and, if necessary, change their clothes. They are little treasures and he would like to see them playing the part. Minimise all noise. At the time of his arrival, eliminate all noise of the washer, dryer or vacuum. Try to encourage the children to be quiet.

- Be happy to see him.

- Greet him with a warm smile and show sincerity in your desire to please him.

- Listen to him. You may have a dozen important things to tell him, but the moment of his arrival is not the time. Let him talk first – remember, his topics of conversation are more important than yours.

- Make the evening his. Never complain if he comes home late or goes out to dinner, or other places of entertainment without you. Instead, try to understand his world of strain and pressure and his very real need to be at home and relax.

- Your goal: Try to make sure your home is a place of peace, order and tranquillity where your husband can renew himself in body and spirit.

- Don't greet him with complaints and problems.

- Don't complain if he's late home for dinner or even if he stays out all night. Count this as minor compared to what he might have gone through that day.

- Make him comfortable. Have him lean back in a comfortable chair or have him lie down in the bedroom. Have a cool or warm drink ready for him.

- Arrange his pillow and offer to take off his shoes. Speak in a low, soothing and pleasant voice.

- Don't ask him questions about his actions or question his judgment or integrity. Remember, he is the master of the house and as such will always exercise his will with fairness and truthfulness. You have no right to question him.

- A good wife always knows her place.

that Norma's job as a wife was harder than mine until I looked up what "laying down your life" actually means. I believe it goes back to the illustration of the chicken and the pig. Who sacrificed more for the ham and eggs for your breakfast this morning? The pig sacrificed more, because he died. The chicken simply laid a few eggs and continued throughout her day.

Let's take a deeper look at what Ephesians 5 truly means by serving each other in marriage.

Service and Submission

For many couples the issue of submission is a hot-button topic, but I'd like to show you how to understand this passage in a fresh way. Ephesians 5:22 commands, "Wives, submit to your husbands as to the Lord." In other words, women serve by submitting. But men are called to die and truly lay down their lives for their wives. You won't be able to do any of these commands using your own measly love and power. But keep in mind, these are God's words, and He'll empower you to keep them.

It's important to note that Ephesians 5:22 is a statement of order in the home, not a statement of value or worth. In God's eyes, both the wife and husband are "coheirs before God." Notice that the Scripture says you can only do this after you submit to Christ and are filled with His Holy Spirit. "Don't be drunk with wine. . . . Instead, be filled with the Holy Spirit" (Eph. 5:18, *NLT*). That filling gives both of you the *desire and the power* to carry out God's order of woman's submission and man's sacrifice.

I (Gary) am convinced that most men who have a plan and know what to do are willing to take the steps needed to build a loving, lasting relationship. The problem is that the average man doesn't know intuitively what it takes to do so—nor does he realize the incredible benefits that a strong relationship at home brings to nearly every area of his life.

For a man, the first place he should check when it comes to building a strong family is the blueprint found in Ephesians 5. In this chapter of the Bible, the man is called to be the "head" of his wife—the primary lover—just as Christ is the Head of the Church and the lover of the Church.

How did Christ lead in love? By serving regardless of the cost. The greatest among us are simply following a pattern Christ set down—namely, serving those He loved and for whom He laid down His life.

Let's take the command for a man to be a loving leader in the home and move it down to the shoe leather level. What does it mean to be the "leader" in a home?

When it comes to "leadership" and headship in the home, one specific guideline is found in Ephesians 5:28-29: "Husbands *ought to love their wives* as their own bodies . . . [for] no one ever hated his own body, but he feeds and cares for it, *just as Christ does the church*" (emphasis added). If we are following the biblical pattern for family leadership, we men are to nurture and cherish our wives (and children). We do so in the same manner we nurture and cherish our own bodies . . . just as Christ nurtures and cherishes the Church.

When a husband makes that important decision to truly honor those entrusted to him, he takes the first step toward being the loving nurturer God meant him to be. As a result, he can see his relationships begin to blossom before his eyes and grow. As the man, just think about what you do for yourself every day: you get up, shower, eat, dress, and so on. Make a list of what you do every day, from getting up to lying down at night. You and I get to do the same for our mate and children; that is, we make sure they are taken care of exactly as we are.

I often receive pushback when I address this topic of biblical roles in marriage, but we cannot allow our modern culture to define the way we read the Bible. We must use the Scriptures to seek God's guidance and understand the roles He created in marriage for our welfare. Though women may flinch at the command for wives to submit, it's essential to look at the Greek meaning of the word "submit," which is *huppatasso*, meaning to "fall in line under the leadership of another." *Huppatasso* is actually a military term and implies the idea, "I see and respect and honor the leadership structure that has been put in place in my home."

For men, the command is much fiercer. Ephesians 5:25 instructs, "Husbands, love your wives, just as Christ loved the church and gave himself up for her." In other words, husbands are to lay down their lives in service.

Notice that this verse doesn't say that wives are commanded to submit to *all* men. Whenever I do premarital counseling, I'll often have to remind a man that his fiancée does not have to submit to him. Nowhere in Scripture does it say that girlfriends have to submit to boyfriends or fiancés. The Scripture in Ephesians 5 addresses only the married state.

The number-one question I get from guys in the area of marriage is, *How do I get my wife to submit?* Sometimes men think they have to tell or remind their wives that they're the leader in the relationship. But that's like Eisenhower saying, "Guys, I am the leader of the Allied Command, so you have to listen to me!" Who wants to follow that? No one.

Husbands become leaders of the home by leading for the welfare of the family and faithfully loving their wives like Christ loved the Church and gave Himself up for her. Though there's a mysterious nature to this idea, and it's not easy to always understand, I am so thankful for the created order in marriage that God has placed in Scripture.

So how do you fulfill this created order in your marriage?

The *Self-focused marriage* serves to be noticed and appreciated. The *Christ-focused marriage* serves when the act is overlooked and unappreciated.

The *Self-focused marriage* serves for applause and reward. The *Christ-focused marriage* is discreet in its acts of love.

The *Self-focused marriage* is guided and ruled by feelings. The *Christ-focused marriage* serves even when the feelings are not there.

Practice Appreciation

One of the best ways to love your spouse is to show thankfulness. How do you know if gratefulness is abounding in your heart? Do an attitude check. Are you complaining regularly? Do you grumble about your spouse? Are you tempted to whine? Do you find yourself nagging your spouse about what's left undone rather than applaud his or her efforts?

For me (Ted), there's nothing I enjoy hearing more coming out of my five-year-old daughter's mouth than, "You're the bestest daddy ever!"

I usually hear those words after I've purchased her a Build-A-Bear. Her affirmation makes me wish I could buy her a truckload of the fuzzy animals. My daughter's words remind me of what our heavenly Father longs to hear from you and me. God wants us to know and recognize that He is "the bestest Daddy ever!" When we focus on the goodness and generosity of God, we can't help but become more appreciative and grateful, which spills over onto our family.

So spend some time focusing on God and thanking Him for all He's done for you. Then spend some time thanking God for all the good things He's given you in your spouse. Over the next few days, express your appreciation to your spouse in words of affirmation and encouragement.

Here are 10 ways to show appreciation and honor to your spouse:

1. *Make an effort to remember your spouse's past requests and desires and begin to fulfill them when possible.* A close friend of mine told me his wife had just done something that made him feel very special. Several weeks before this, he had remarked to her, "I wish I could watch just one football game from start to finish without getting interrupted." One day as he started to turn on a game, his wife came into the den, took both kids by the hand and said, "Let's go up for a nap." After putting them to bed, she came in and said, "I'm going to go shopping now, and I hope you're able to enjoy this game without any interruptions. I've taken the phone off the hook so you won't be disturbed by any calls." What amazed him was that his wife remembered his comment from several weeks before and had looked for the opportunity to do something about it. In appreciation, he began to work on some long overdue household projects.

2. *Hug and kiss each other in front of the children.* The power of NSTs (nonsexual touches) says, "I love you and am thrilled to be married to you." When your wife is carrying a laundry basket around the house, stop her. Set the basket on the floor. Hug her. Then pick up the basket and deliver it to its destination. (*Side note: If you don't pick up the basket for her, it kind of spoils the whole idea here.*)

3. *Look for the occasional opportunity to draw attention to your mate's positive qualities when you're with other people.* For example, praise

your husband to your children, calling attention to his positive character qualities. If you are with friends and he says something worthwhile, tell him you think it makes a lot of sense, and ask him to explain it further. Or, relate to friends and relatives a specific incident in the past week that highlights one of his positive qualities. For example: "John is so considerate of my feelings. The other day I hadn't said a word about how I felt, but he could tell I was down. He came over and put his arms around me. Then he told me he knew I was troubled and asked how he could help." I (Gary) can't begin to express how good I feel inside when people occasionally tell me something positive my wife has said about me. It makes me feel appreciated—I want to go home and put my arms around her as soon as I can!

4. *Don't let two days pass without expressing appreciation for at least one thing your mate has said or done during those 48 hours.* Just a reminder: Don't forget how much nicer it is to be with people who make you feel special.

5. *Make an effort to gain an appreciation for your mate's occupation.* Many people are frustrated with their job, feeling that no one really appreciates their worth or value, or their talents and abilities. When you appreciate what your mate does, you may become his/her *only* hope for achieving genuine self-worth. Until your mate really believes that he/she is worth something, he or she will have difficulty focusing attention on the worth of others—including you. Don't ever belittle your mate's job. Nothing destroys self-esteem more than to hear your mate cutting down your efforts. Though you may not criticize his/her efforts, you may belittle by disinterest. Engage in conversations

about your mate's workplace. Remember the names of colleagues and friends. Connect the dots when a story today reminds you of something that coworker did or said months or even years ago. Remembering the history of your spouse's workplace says, "I've been listening, and I am engaged." This shows great appreciation for what your mate does!

6. *Genuinely desire and seek your spouse's forgiveness when you offend.* Both men and women tend to avoid those who offend them. (One of the most common complaints children make about their parents is that parents never admit they are wrong.) The key to wiping the slate clean with your spouse is not saying "I'm sorry"—that's a phrase even children exploit to avoid a spanking. When someone has offended us, we usually don't want to hear a glib "I'm sorry." We want to know that the person realizes he or she was wrong and has hurt us. I believe there are a lot of "wrong ways" to ask forgiveness. They are wrong because they do not bring us into harmony with the person we have offended and they may not communicate how we value the person. One of the best ways I've found to ask forgiveness is, unfortunately, the hardest and the least creative. All it requires is that you go to your husband (or wife), look into his eyes and say, "I was wrong in what I said or did. Can you forgive me?" Two things will happen when you ask for forgiveness in this way. First, your spouse may desire to restore the relationship and will be more prepared to forgive you; and second, your apology is likely to exert pressure on your spouse to ask for forgiveness in the future whenever he/she has offended you. As a side benefit, it makes your mate feel important—you are say-

ing indirectly that you care too much to leave him/her with hurt feelings.

7. *Declare a moratorium on pessimism.* If your tendency is to always see the negative side, declare a full 24-hour period when every word that proceeds from your mouth is positive. The following story vividly portrays two opposite ways of looking at the same thing . Which farmer is most like you? The story is told of two farmers. One was a pessimist, the other an optimist. The optimist would say, "Wonderful sunshine." The pessimist would respond, "Yes, but I'm afraid it's going to scorch the crops." The optimist would say, "Fine rain." The pessimist would respond, "Yes, but I'm afraid we're going to have a flood." One day the optimist said to the pessimist, "Have you seen my new bird dog? He's the finest money can buy." The pessimist said, "You mean that mutt I saw penned up behind your house. Didn't look like much to me." The two went hunting with the dog the next day. They shot some ducks. The ducks landed in the pond. The optimist ordered his dog to get the ducks. The dog obediently responded and instead of swimming in the water the dog walked on top of the water, retrieved the ducks, and walked back on top of the water with the ducks. The optimist turned to his friend and said, "Now, what do you think of that?" The pessimist replied, "Hmm, he can't swim, can he?"

8. *Guard your fun activities.* If every outing you take ends up in heated conversation, declare a break from serious conversation. You need to experience periods of time when you don't take yourselves so seriously. Learn to laugh with each other. Lighthearted evenings are great stress relievers. Try to make all of your date nights and trips together free of arguments.

Sign a short contract between you that there will be no fights or angry arguments while you're having fun and kicking back together.

9. *Focus on the little acts of kindness, not just the "biggies."* A lot of guys think their wives need to be blown away by some incredible gift or act, but in fact a little thank-you goes a long way.

10. *Praise your spouse at least once a day.* Daily appreciation is so important to keep your marriage from developing a vacuum of intimacy. Promise yourself—not your mate—because he/she might develop expectations and be hurt if you forget. Begin by learning to verbalize your thoughts of appreciation. Plus, this is a simple way of adding to the "5 to 1" positive experiences.

Kind words go a long way to building a healthy marriage; so remember:

- Your spouse may be unreasonable and difficult at times; love anyway.
- If you choose to serve, you may be accused of having ulterior motives; serve anyway.
- Your service today will be forgotten tomorrow; serve anyway.
- Give to your mate without reservation and you may be judged as holier-than-thou; give anyway.

In the next chapter, we're going to explore the importance of commitment in a relationship and look at three attitudes regarding unresolved issues . . . a couple's underestimation of their differences . . . and issues of unforgiveness that may be undermining your marriage without your even realizing it!

Here are some typical statements wives have told me they enjoy hearing:

- "What a meal! The way that you topped that casserole with sour cream and cheese . . . M-m-m-m, that was delicious."
- Put little notes on the refrigerator like, "I loved the way you looked last night."
- "Our kids are really blessed to have a mother like you. You take such good care of them."
- "I like that dress, but I prefer what's in it."
- "Do I like your hairstyle? I'd like any hairstyle you have just because it's on you."
- "I'd love to take you out tonight just to show you off."
- "Honey, you've worked so hard. Why don't you sit down and rest for a while before dinner? I can wait."

Here are some typical statements husbands have told me they enjoy hearing:

- "Hey, honey, why don't you call some buddies this weekend to hang out. You deserve it."
- "I'll take care of the kids tonight; you go watch the game."
- "Thanks for letting me go shopping this weekend. I appreciated the little extra spending money."
- "The yard looks phenomenal. Who taught you how to stripe a yard?"
- "I look forward to you being home tonight."
- "There's no rush getting home, I've got everything under control. Stay a bit longer if you need to get something done."
- "The kids wanted me to call and tell you that you are the best daddy in the whole wide world."

FROM GARYSMALLEY.COM

This question was sent to our website by a woman who needs advice on sorting out boundary issues with family and friends.

Q: *My husband and I have been married for nine years, and we have three great children. He is a great husband and father. Last year his job transferred us back to our hometown. At first we thought it would be kind of fun to be with parents, family and friends again. However, we did not plan on all of the expectations placed on us by family and friends. Life is busy enough with a family of five, but now we have extended family expecting our time each week. What suggestions do you have to maintain a strong marriage and family time without making our extended family mad?*

A: One word comes to mind while reading your story: Boundaries! When counseling young couples, I often take them to Genesis 2:24, "For this reason a man will leave his father and mother and be united to his wife, and they will become one flesh." We call this "The Leaving and Cleaving" principle. A couple cannot experience oneness until they have drawn strong boundaries with any and all people who would affect their unity. That starts with your parents. I have heard mothers often say on the day of their daughter's wedding, "I don't feel as though I am losing a daughter today, but more like I am gaining a son." In many ways, the success of the marriage rests on the couples' commitment to leaving family and friends.

This does not mean that you do not go home for holidays or never have family or friends over for dinner. It simply means that you now have a new family. This new family will create new traditions, enjoy new vacation spots and fill a new schedule. Extended family must make room for that. Trust me, I'm a dad and grandfather. I have learned how to give my children room to breathe. It is not always easy.

You cannot be responsible for the expectations placed on you by your extended family and friends. With grace and respect, identify and communicate to them the best days of the week to call or suggest getting together. Explain your need to put your children and each other first in order to maintain a strong marriage and emotional health in your children. The better you communicate clear boundaries, the less you will stress over frustrations you experience with each group dinner or activity with family.

What happens if you do not create some boundaries? You will stuff your frustration and anger until, like a volcano, you erupt. Take personal responsibility for your actions. Get together with your husband and discuss your needs for space and time with your kids. Together, create acceptable boundaries for both of you. Then communicate those boundaries as a couple to family and friends.

CHAPTER 9

COMMITTED FOREVER

I (Ted) will never forget visiting my extended family in Florida several summers ago. My family knew that Amy and I were embracing the marriage and family ministry calling. This meant that I was asked all sorts of questions at family events. As I was talking with several family and friends about their former marriages, my cousin Greg stood silently close by. With one foot on the back bumper of the car, his elbow on the hood and beer in hand, he was in deep thought. The conversation lasted for an hour before Greg finally spoke up.

Single, and not seriously dating anyone at the time, Greg simply said, "Ted, I have to be able to answer one question before I marry."

Taking the bait, I said, "What's that?"

"Am I ready to spend the next 6 to 8 years of my life with this woman?"

Everyone laughed, and for a brief moment it sounded like a reasonable question. But it's not! In this chapter, we're going to look at 17 healthy expectations you should have for your marriage. These expectations are not just to cover a few years with a spouse; they are a commitment for life. Who would say, "I'd like to marry you for just a few years and then trade you in for a new model"?

In chapter 10, we'll look at what it means to take full responsibility for the commitment you made on your wedding day.

Finally, in chapter 11, we'll look at how to give your marriage a complete makeover.

Seventeen Healthy Expectations for Your Marriage

My cousin Greg's question is not really a joke. It represents the twenty-first century mindset for marriage. As you read in chapter 3, my generation is not as committed to the idea of marriage as is the Builder and Boomer generations.

With all the expectations we've discussed in this book, the tendency may be to bring all of your expectations down to zero. Maybe you're thinking, "No expectations make for a great marriage." This simply is not true! Do you remember the list of expectations from chapter 1 that probably need to go out the window? Well, here are the expectations that rank as a "10" in both the "expectation" and the "reality" column:

1. *The husband as spiritual leader.* Praying together, having daily devotions and attending church regularly.
2. *Bragging on each other in public.* While dating, you bragged each other up to family and friends. You showed a picture of your love every chance you got. So this will continue throughout your marriage.
3. *Courtesy.* Open doors, push back a chair, offer a jacket on a cold night.
4. *Kindness.* Exchange uplifting, positive words in your communication with each other.
5. *Patience.* Endure with one another.
6. *Freedom from addiction.* Substance abuse, alcohol, pornography will not destroy our marriage.
7. *Unconditional love.* My spouse will love me even when I am going through difficult times emotionally.
8. *Tenderness/gentleness.* Our words will defuse anger and encourage each other.
9. *Validation.* My spouse will understand my fear, frustration or hurt. Listening to me will always triumph over solving my problems.
10. *Together forever.* We will never leave each other. The "D" word (divorce) will never be an option for us. We are together until one of us lays the other in the arms of Jesus.

11. *Grace and forgiveness.* The spirit of forgiveness will always exist in our home. We will not judge each other because we are both imperfect and make mistakes. There will be much room for error.

12. *Devotions and prayer.* We will set a goal to memorize at least 50 great top verses in Scripture and meditate together daily on these verses, hearing the meaning of each verse. These verses will give us the top 10 most important beliefs that Christ directs us to cultivate within our hearts. We will pray at every meal.

13. *Eyes-for-no-other faithfulness.* His eyes do not wander from me and to another for prolonged, lustful thoughts.

14. *Admission of mistakes.* My spouse will always be forthcoming with mistakes and character defects in his/her life. When offenses occur, my spouse will seek forgiveness from me.

15. *Cared for when sick.* In the dating years, did he or she prepare get-well baskets stuffed with tissue, soup, candles or a favorite magazine? That mercy will continue throughout the years of marriage.

16. *United front.* No one will ever be able to put me down to my mate. No parent, family member or friend will get away with slandering me to him/her. We will remain in harmony and united in a win-win agreement with all arguments.

17. *Protection.* My spouse will take a bullet for me if necessary. Sounds in the middle of the night will be quickly investigated and resolved.

These expectations are just a fraction of the list but they move beyond reasonable to being placed in the healthy expectations category. They demand a "10" and nothing less. When we have given this assessment to couples, it grieves me (Ted) to see a spouse put anything lower than a "10" on expectations such as "freedom from addiction," "together forever" and "marital fidelity." What that tells me is the person has been hurt before. And to keep from going through that pain again, the person will lower his or her expectations. Don't believe the lie that says lower expectations will lessen pain in the event of separation, unfaithfulness or divorce.

All too often, people marry before acquiring the knowledge and skills necessary to take care of their mate—before acquiring the knowledge to meet his or her emotional, mental and physical needs. One of the ironies in our society is that a person has to have four years of training to receive a plumber's license but absolutely no training for a marriage license. Our educational system doesn't even require communication courses basic to the meaningful development of any relationship. I was certainly among the untrained when I married. It has taken my wife, Norma, and my friends many years to help me become a more loving husband.

It is typical for a man to marry without knowing how to talk to his wife. Some men don't even know that their wives need intimate communication. Often a man is completely unaware that his wife may have a sensitive side. He doesn't realize that a woman's home, children, family and friends are an interwoven part of her identity.

Many women step into marriage equally handicapped. They don't understand that admiration is to a man what romance is to a woman. They don't understand that a man generally relies on reasoning rather than intuitive sensitivity.

All the things that undermine marriage can be summed up in three categories: (1) unresolved issues from the past; (2) underestimation of differences; and (3) unforgiveness of past mistakes.

Unresolved Issues from the Past

Marriage is simply two imperfect people committing to live life together forever. In marriage, a man and woman go through the mysterious, holy metamorphosis of becoming one flesh. A lot of people believe that marriage *creates* problems, but actually marriage *reveals* problems. Marriage exposes the issues that lay below the surface in all of our lives. If I (Ted) had not married Amy, I would still have a lot of unresolved issues in my life. Simply living life together as a couple—with work, a mortgage and children—has allowed hidden issues in my life to rise to the surface.

Dan and Janel did not have one relationship expectation over a "5" on their list. This was the third marriage for Dan and the second for Janel. As I met with them in counseling, they were defeated. For them it boiled down to "we are expected to get married," but a "great marriage" is no longer possible.

Dan was very angry and Janel was codependent. Both had negative beliefs about who they were. These unresolved issues followed them into every job and marriage. Neither Dan nor Janel had seen models of healthy marriage while growing up. Both came from divorced homes. Dan was left to raise himself. He was given no instruction on boundaries. This turned from frustration to hatred in his teen and young adult years.

Janel had the unresolved issue in her heart that she was "ugly and unworthy," placed there through years of abuse. This unresolved issue in turn produced negative rules that governed her behavior:

1. Don't be intimate with your husband. *Who would want me anyway?*
2. Don't bother with makeup or nice clothes. *Nothing I do will make me attractive.*
3. Don't give yourself to this guy who says he loves you. *I'll just get hurt in the end.*

These rules controlled every aspect of Janel's life. Her expectations, her actions and her decisions all flowed from her unresolved issues. It didn't matter that her belief about herself was not true. She was quite attractive and intelligent. But her experiences had embedded into her mind the belief that she was an undesirable nobody; and that belief formed her view of who she was and what she was like. Have you known someone who glances downward rather than meet your eyes, or looks so shy and uncomfortable being in your presence? When I have had the chance to become close friends with very shy people, I have discovered that some of these people believe they are stupid, unattractive or unworthy of having a close friend.

Dan's anger was built upon his unresolved issues that "Life is too hard and no one is looking out for me." His behavior, at times, was belligerent and flowed from these core thoughts:

1. I'm going to step on whoever I need to for survival.
2. I work so hard but never seem to get ahead.
3. Life is all about going it alone.

How do you suppose these deep-seated beliefs would affect a marriage? Day by day, each partner filters the other's behavior through what he or she believes. This can quickly turn a mate into an opponent rather than a teammate. Suppose you believe that your mate is responsible for meeting all your needs. What happens when he or she doesn't do this? Your reaction will be a response to what you believe should be happening. To you it will not seem complex or filtered or skewed in any way. It will usually be automatic and accompanied by emotion, and you will experience it simply as thought. But if you analyze it and trace its origin, you will find that it is really an expression of what you believe.

Dan and Janel are still together and are working on changing the lies by which they've been living. It may take years to change, but that is okay. That is why we are talking about commitment. You grow together in terms of years. You need to start thinking in terms of a lifetime, because that's what it takes to form the marriage bond.

Couples need a lifetime commitment to love each other more deeply, forgive each other more readily and grow in unexpected ways. The shaping and refining that goes on in marriage is in our best interests. Instead of being frustrated by it, we should celebrate God's providence and plan in bringing us a mate that makes us become more like Jesus.

Underestimation of Differences

You've heard the saying "opposites attract," but in marriage, it's usually "opposites attack." During premarital counseling, couples will often talk about all they have in common. This is because in the first stage of a relationship couples tend to overemphasize the things they have in common and underestimate their differences.

While dating, I (Gary) assumed that Norma would always love my fun-loving, easygoing, big-dreaming personality. I appreciated her uniqueness and skill with numbers and details. While we were dating, the contrast of our differences were fun and gave us plenty to talk about.

Once we were married, the similarities got downplayed and the differences were magnified. Now, 43 years later, our personalities have not changed. As we thoroughly discussed in chapter 4, Norma and I are very different. Marriage is only one part of it. Working with your mate has a whole new set of challenges. My personality only sees big-picture possibilities, and Norma's personality loves the nuts and bolts of how it all will work. Underestimated differences can create a great deal of tension.

Marriage is much like a boat in which the differences between a couple are like icebergs floating up ahead. They can see the surface of the berg, but what they can't see may be 10 times larger. Overlooking or underestimating differences can sink them if they're not careful.

Do not neglect the differences between you and your mate. Have a reasonable estimate of each one's differences and how they play out in your marriage and cause disharmony if you're always trying to get each other to think exactly alike. The really good news is that differences viewed as making up for what each other lack can be one of the most important strengths of your marriage.

Unforgiven Mistakes

When you refuse to forgive and move beyond the glitches in your marriage, you plant seeds of resentment and unforgiveness. Eventually bitter roots set in, and you will find your relationship struggling to thrive.

A healthy marriage requires an atmosphere of forgiveness nurtured by the ability to love and let go of the past. First Corinthians 13 tells us that love keeps no record of wrong. If you rehash the mistakes and mishaps of your spouse, you'll find discontentment and anger growing in your heart. Before you know it, you'll only catch your spouse doing wrong things—and missing all the moments your spouse is doing everything right.

I often think, *If Norma forgave me, then she would be over this by now!* This is not realistic. If I've done something extremely hurtful, and I need to seek her forgiveness, then I can't expect the healing to happen immediately. It takes time. Just because you have earnestly sought forgiveness and forgiveness has been given does not mean there will not be consequences for your actions.

I think back periodically on my first several years of marriage and am just sickened by the things I said to Norma. I said things that I am too embarrassed to share with you in print. I don't dwell on them, but sometimes they just pop up in my memory and I'm reminded about what a jerk I was at times during our first year together.

I think these remembrances are one way that God keeps us humble. Remembering a mistake does not mean that it is unforgiven. Forgiving and forgetting are mutually exclusive.

Take Responsibility for Your Promise

When you stood at the altar and said, "For better or for worse, for richer or for poorer, in sickness and in health, until death do us part," you made a promise to work through issues with your mate until either Jesus returns or one of you dies. Here are several ways that you can do this.

1. Make a Mutual Commitment

First, you need to make a mutual commitment to the slow process of learning how to relate. I (Gary) have found that a relationship doesn't remain at the same place year after year. You're both growing and improving or your relationship is going downhill. If you're not studying and learning about one another, then your relationship tends to go flat. When it comes to the differences between men and women, Norma and I made the commitment that we could continue to grow. On one occasion we decided to fast together.

Here's how Norma tells the rest of the story: "We prayed, fasted and read the Word together from Friday night through Saturday afternoon. We also took some time to work on our marriage goals. It was like we were having our own spiritual revival. However, I was not enjoying myself because I felt forced into fasting. And by late Saturday afternoon, I was emotionally drained and starving. So we took a break by walking around an indoor mall. Unfortunately, there was food everywhere, but I couldn't have any because we'd agreed not to eat until Monday morning. So we went back to the hotel and continued fasting and working on our marriage goals. By Saturday evening, I was miserable. I was so hungry that it became difficult for me to concentrate. So around 10:00 p.m. Saturday night, I finally pleaded, 'I've got to get food . . . I'm done!'

" 'Why should we give up now since we only have one more day?' Gary demanded. Because he had fasted before, he knew that on the third day you're not as hungry. But I was done!

" 'I don't know what you're going to do,' I snapped. 'But I'm going to eat.' I enjoyed an egg omelet, toast and hash browns, despite Gary's continuous glare. He had nothing but water.

"The next day, Gary realized we had to do the very things we had talked about through the weekend. We had to forgive and love one another. We also had to accept each other as unique individuals. After we did these things, we went home in harmony."

Sometimes you will try new things as you grow together that won't work as well as you anticipated. But if your goal is to continue to learn and grow, adjustments can be made as needed. The best way to help you and your husband have success during this slow process is actually the third step (willingness to help your spouse up when he/she has "fallen").

2. Agree to Join a Marriage Support Group

Small groups help couples keep their promises. Participation in a small group can provide three important helps for your marriage. First, groups give support—which means you get a chance to be encouraged and prayed for on a weekly basis. This provides additional energy to keep moving toward fulfilling the promises you've made to each other. Second, support groups provide accountability. What's great about accountability is that since you know someone will be asking you how your week went, you're constantly working on your promises.

The third reason for being in a small group is that men seem to learn best by watching other men interact with their mates and with each other. For example, if your husband came from a home where his father wasn't a good model, small groups can provide healthy role models.

We've found that the most effective small group is one in which you all agree on the direction. I encourage you to develop some specific goals so you don't end up with simply a "social" group.

There are very powerful results that come from being in a loving support group. Make sure your group is healthy in the sense that one person is not controlling the group—stifling your ability to grow closer to the Lord.

3. Be Willing to Help Your Spouse Get up When He/She Falls

One of the easiest things for me to do, even when we are having an argument, is to pause and realize all is not lost. We may have fallen, but we're not a total failure.

Delays at airports can absolutely wear us out. And at our age, connecting flights can almost kill us. Recently, we were connecting to the last flight out of Dallas to Springfield, Missouri, and we knew we were cutting it close. As we got on the shuttle to get from the D terminal to the B terminal, we were just a tad bit snippy with each other. But please cut us some slack: it was 10 PM and two hours past our bedtime. As we boarded the shuttle, all the seats were taken, and we had to stand with all of our bags. Are you picturing two almost-seventy year olds, exhausted and trying to stay happy? As the shuttle left the station, Norma was not braced for the departure. You know what's coming . . . it all happened in slow motion as Norma fell flat to the floor. Looking up at me, she saw my smile. She then smiled. All we could do was laugh.

We didn't make the flight. Now we had to find a hotel. Instead of thinking everything was lost, Norma reminded me how many times we'd been successful. I knew we weren't perfect, but I knew we could keep moving. In a sense, that's like a small group. When you encourage your spouse to look at the overall picture, you give him or her energy.

4. Praise Your Spouse

Finally, praise any action your mate does that brings energy or joy to you or your family. A man returning from Promise Keepers decided that he needed to be more affectionate with his wife. One day, while he was showering, he realized he'd forgotten his towel. As he jumped across the hall to grab a towel, he saw his wife in the kitchen. Trying to keep his new promise, he decided to surprise her with a meaningful hug! So he ran into the kitchen, threw his arms around his wife and shouted, "Honey, I love you!"

Everything was perfect until he heard some noise behind him. He was horrified as he turned to see a neighbor lady sitting at the table!

Although this wife was very embarrassed, she needs to recognize and praise the husband's positive effort. It's like a bank account. Words of praise are like $1,000,000 deposits. Every time you deposit something in your husband's account, it gives him energy. However, every time you criticize, much-needed energy is withdrawn from the account. Unfortunately, if at the end of the month your relationship has more withdrawals than deposits, you risk bankruptcy in his emotional account. As you help your husband keep his promises to your marriage, try to keep a much higher balance in the area of encouraging words.

The Marriage Makeover

As you read about what can undermine a marriage, you may find somewhere between one and four factors that are contributing to your marriage being less than its best. The good news is that it's never too late to turn things around! Even if you're at the point of calling it quits, you can revolutionize your relationship by accepting personal responsibility for your actions and attitudes, trusting God for a miracle, dealing with unresolved hurts, and getting Christian counseling.

Accept Personal Responsibility

In Galatians 6:5, Paul states that "each one should carry his own load." In other words, we are responsible for our own conduct. That means you have to stop pointing a finger at your spouse and instead go stand in front of a mirror. Take a long hard look at yourself, your attitudes and your actions. In Galatians 6:2, just three verses earlier, we like to cling to the words, "Carry each other's burdens, and in this way you will fulfill the law of Christ." We prefer to share blame, fault and responsibility with others. It makes the "burden" lighter. But Scripture makes it clear that there are loads we are responsible for on our own. And part of that load is our words, thoughts, feelings and actions.

Trust God for a Miracle

Unfortunately, I meet couples who are in the process of getting a divorce and both spouses are already rebounding by dating other people. They're not giving God time to do a miracle. If you are at the point of considering divorce, don't turn your affections to another person. Keep focused on God and the restoration of your marriage. Nothing is beyond His power. Nothing is beyond His ability to reconcile or redeem. Remember that with God all things are possible. So don't give up yet!

Even if you've been trying to restore your marriage for years, there's still hope with God's help. Turn it over to Him. Ask God to do something that you haven't been able to do. We see miracles all of the time in our ministry. Our friends at the National Institute of Marriage see miracles every week in their Intensive Marriage Couseling program. No more than five couples in a week come into the Marriage Intensive to spend four days (32 hours) to save their marriage. The criteria are simple. They must be desperate and open to a miracle.

These couples come from all over the world and have either divorced, separated or filed divorce papers and are about to sign. They are done with their mate and marriage. I love how the National Institute of Marriage uses the children of Israel and their plight and exodus from Egypt as a parallel for each couple's situation.

It starts in Egypt: bondage. It then leads to the Red Sea where God performs one of the greatest miracles of the Bible. He parts the seas, gives His people passage on dry land, and swallows up the Egyptian army.

When we ask a couple, "Do you believe in miracles?" their answer is usually always "Yes!"

"Do you believe God miraculously saved His people from Egyptian captivity?"

"Yes!"

"Do you believe God miraculously opened the Red Sea and allowed His people to cross on dry land?"

"Absolutely!"

"Do you believe God can save your marriage?"

Some have answered, "No!"

Maybe you, too, believe God can miraculously save the Israelites from the Egyptians but cannot save your marriage. If God saved His people, I know He can save your marriage. Start with a personal revival in your heart and life. Let the miracle start with you and your heart. Commit to doing whatever it takes. Turning your marriage around may cost you everything; but whatever it takes, it's worth it! Don't get tired of doing what is good (see Gal. 6:9). Don't get discouraged. Don't give up.

Deal with Unresolved Hurts

Every good relationship will experience its fair share of hurts. When you put two people together, no matter how much they love each other, they will do things that hurt each other. Even when unintentional, these emotional hurts and pains are very real.

What unresolved hurts do you have in your life? Are you harboring any anger or bitterness toward your spouse? Are there issues you can't let go? Are there small interactions or any statements from your spouse that result in an emotional outburst from you? If so, these are signs of unforgiveness in your life. You may be harboring anger or resentment without even realizing it.

So how do you deal with unresolved hurts? First, you need to ask for forgiveness. James 5:16 says, "Confess your faults one to another" (*KJV*). For Amy and me (Ted), this has brought a great deal of marital satisfaction into our lives. It's opened the door to communicate vulnerably and honestly about our struggles and mistakes. On more days that I can count, I'll turn to my wife and say, "Amy, I need you to forgive me for . . ." This helps nurture a spirit of forgiveness in my own heart.

Second, you need to offer forgiveness. The Bible instructs us to bear with one another and forgive whatever grievances you may have against one another. In other words, forgive just as the Lord forgave you (see Col. 3:13-14). Forgiveness isn't just something you ask for; it's also something you extend to others.

My (Gary's) wife recently found out from her doctor that she has three ulcers. She jokes with me that she can tie each ulcer back to one of my huge dreams for the future. Shortly after finding out about the ulcers I criticized her approach to a problem in our office. The worst part about it was that I criticized her in front of the staff. We did not have lunch together that afternoon. That night I sought forgiveness for the umpteenth time in our marriage, but this time the response was a bit different. She placed her hand over her stomach and said, "I forgive you." She always does!

Get Christian Counseling

If you had a painful, large kidney stone, you wouldn't walk around saying, "Oh, no, I'm just going to let it go because it costs about $6,000 to have the surgery and I don't want to spend the money." You wouldn't care if it cost $20,000. You would get the help you needed!

Yet all too often couples are walking around doubled over emotionally from their unhealthy marriage situation. The pain is crippling, yet they're not willing to get help or pay for it. If your marriage is in trouble, money should not be an issue. You can find the money. You can borrow it. You can learn to live on less. Your marriage is too important. Get help and get it fast.

We believe in the power of quality, biblically based Christian counseling, much like what is offered by our friends at the National Institute of Marriage. Charlie and Kim had divorce paperwork filed, so the marriage intensive at the institute was their last-ditch effort. Even though they answered yes to the "Do you believe in miracles?" question during the screening, it was a half-hearted response.

On the first day of the Marriage Intensive they didn't even want to sit by each other on the couch. Because five couples are present in the Intensive it really works best when each person sits with his/her spouse. It cuts down on confusion for the two therapists as well. Charlie and Kim agreed to sit by each other, but their body language said, "Don't touch me!" Would you believe me if I told you they were holding hands by the fourth day? Well, they were! How awesome is that! God does do miracles, and sometimes He works through others to make it happen.

I have become friends with many of the therapists at the National Institute of Marriage, and I call each one of them "Moses." Just as God used Moses to part the Red Sea during the Israelites' exodus from slavery in Egypt, He uses godly men and women to work His miracles within marriages today.

Final words: *Get help! Get counseling!*

Your marriage is worth saving, and it's worth fighting for. With God's grace and strength, you can fulfill the commitment you made on your wedding day and be a testimony of redemption and renewal to those around you.

In the next chapter, we're going to explore what it means to finish well. We're going to tell you how to ensure your marriage stays strong to the end. Then we're going to explore the real heart of commitment and leave you with an unforgettable story of what it means to truly love until the end.

FROM GARYSMALLEY.COM

This question was sent to our website by a man tempted with the allure of divorce.

Q: *I don't understand what's happened to my marriage. What seemed to be so right before we got married has turned out very, very wrong. I am wondering if I missed God's will. I know that everybody has problems, but I thought because I was a Christian, my marriage would be different. Before we got married, we thought we had a lot in common, but it is now very clear that we have very little in common, especially since my mate doesn't care about growing spiritually like I do. I keep wondering if maybe the person God wanted me to marry is still out there somewhere. I fantasize about other people I might have married and I'm constantly comparing my spouse to others. Maybe I should divorce and start searching again. All I am sure of is this: I am deeply disappointed in my marriage and I don't know what to do. What went wrong?*

A: First, I don't believe there is only one right person out there for you, and you didn't find her. Biblically, there isn't a Scripture that says there is one person that God chose for you before the foundations of the earth. So don't buy into that myth.

Second, we have an issue in this country: Divorce is too quick and it happens too fast. Our culture makes it look easy. But it's not. You cannot jump out of one marriage, thinking the grass is greener on the other side of the fence and things will be better if you hop over to that side. The problems you have in this marriage will more than likely follow you to the next.

God does not like divorce, but neither does He like crummy marriages. That's why you need to make every effort to improve your relationship with your wife. That begins by taking a good, hard look at yourself. What attitudes and habits of reacting do you need to change? What work does God need to do in your heart? How can you serve, encourage and offer words of affirmation to your spouse? None of this is easy to do, but the work will reap a good harvest for you and your wife.

There's nothing like the helplessness of feeling that there's no one on earth to turn to. As Christians, we may often *fret* that way, but the reality is that we can always turn to the most powerful, influential Person in the whole universe and totally depend on Him. He is waiting to help you if you will sincerely and humbly ask Him. By walking with God through these valleys in your marriage, you can forge a bond with Him that the "good times" simply can't produce. Such dark times inspired David to write: "The LORD is my shepherd, I shall not want. . . . *Though I walk through the valley of the shadow of death,* I will fear no evil, for you are with me" (Ps. 23:1,4, emphasis added). Talk about bonding! David was a man whose heart cleaved to God's because he had faced the fires, and yet God saw him through.

Finally, get help! As you seek out God's help, don't forget that God works through His people. Find a Christian counselor in your area who can help you sort through issues and get you back on the track of marriage God designed for you.

CHAPTER 10

FINISHING WELL

Staying alive feels like a full-time job for Norma and me. Weekly doctors visits, special socks to keep our feet from swelling, dozens of pills and machines to help us sleep at night are all part of our wellness routine.

A few weeks ago, we were just getting started on our evening walk at Branson Landing when Norma doubled over in pain. She has a knee that has been bothering her for years.

"Ouch, my knee is really giving me fits today," Norma said with a shaky voice.

"Let's sit over there on that bench until you feel better; we don't need to do a walk tonight," I said.

"No, I told my knee this morning that it would cooperate or we would have words. So, I don't care how bad this knee hurts, I'll drag it down this landing if I have to. But we're walking no matter what!"

That's why I love her. She's not a quitter; she's never been a quitter. Remember in the last chapter when we challenged you to commit to your mate for life? Keep in mind that we do not want you to just endure a stinky marriage, we want you to love marriage and your mate more and more with each passing year.

Norma and I, despite our failing bodies, are still madly in love. We love doing things together—watching movies, vacationing, walking, eating out. In fact, almost every night feels like a date night. We debrief the day, talk about our dreams and the future and enjoy each other's company. We plan on finishing well together. We plan on growing together until one of us lays the other in the arms of Jesus.

In this chapter, we are going to examine what it means and what it looks like to finish well in a marriage. A great relationship isn't just about starting well—it is also about finishing the race with grace and strength.

Finishing Together

One of the most significant aspects of a healthy marriage is commitment, which includes learning to finish well.

The Progression of a Healthy Marriage

Unmet Expectations ➟ Discovery ➟ Personal Responsibility ➟ **Commitment**

[chapter 1]   [chapters 2–5]   [chapters 6–8]   [chapters 9–11]

In Ecclesiastes 7, Solomon says that it's more important to think about the end than the beginning. He even went as far as to say that if you had the choice between going to a funeral or a party, you should choose the funeral. Why? Because the funeral will teach you a whole lot more about life.

We should not be spending our days and our lives trying to make a great name for ourselves. As followers of Jesus Christ, our goal is to make His name great. We're here to let the world know about Him and one of the greatest testimonies we'll ever give is through the way we love and serve our spouse.

How do you love and serve your spouse in ways that honor your marriage vows? In this chapter, we're going to look at four keys to help you stay strong in your marriage and finish well.

Key No. 1: Choose Character over Happiness

The Bible tells us that Solomon was the wisest man who walked the earth. He had knowledge and insights into everything—from how to manage money to how to maintain the best marriage. And he shared his wisdom with us in the book of Ecclesiastes and the Song of Solomon.

One of my favorite Solomonisms comes from Ecclesiastes 7:3, which says, "Sorrow is better than laughter, because a sad face is good for the heart." That may seem a little depressing at first, but here's what Solomon is really saying: *Pain is meant to shape us.* Pain can be used by God to mold you into His image and allow the fruit of the Spirit to grow in your life in fuller measure.

When I look back on the most painful times of my life, at the time when I was experiencing them, I hated them; I wanted them to pass. I wanted things to change. But now as I look back, I realize those were moments when God was growing me. I was being conformed to the image of Christ.

I know of a pastor in Dallas who shared a story from his early days in ministry. He was working around the clock—burning the candle from both ends as well as in the middle. One day his wife came home with a packed bag and announced, "I'm done; this marriage stinks."

"Give me one more chance, give me one more chance; I will listen," the pastor begged.

"You've never listened," she said. "You have never been concerned about me. Forget you, I'm done."

One of the pastor's friends offered some stinging but truth-filled words, "The Bible is full of information on the way in which we are to live. You love teaching it, but you are not applying it to your life."

The pastor knew he was right.

He spent some time in prayer and fasting and discovered God like he had never experienced Him before. He begged God to give his marriage one more chance. God faithfully answered that prayer. You may recognize the pastor's name: Charles (Chuck) Swindoll.

I (Gary) had the opportunity to speak alongside Chuck Swindoll at an event. I remember looking him in the eyes and saying, "Chuck, you are one of my favorite Christian leaders. Why do you think that is?"

Chuck paused. "Let me get back to you on that."

Later, he said, "The only thing I can think of is pain. I have gone through a lot of pain in life and have wrestled with it. I have had tough times and I have had people not like me. It has made me a leader."

One of my friends in town was recently given a promotion to a new leadership position. I remember looking at him before he accepted the job and saying, "Congratulations! Are you ready to get the snot beat out of you?"

"Well, I was actually just excited about the promotion," he answered. "I didn't think about that."

"Oh, people are going to be mad," I affirmed.

He just looked at me blankly.

A few weeks later he walked into my office, plopped down and announced, "I don't think I am cut out for this."

"You are being cut out for this," I gently but firmly reminded him. This is the road to finishing well:

- God gave you your mate to make you holy, not happy (happiness flows from holiness).
- Marriage is the best tool I know for making you more like Jesus.
- Marriage builds character through patience and endurance.
- Character is not built overnight and neither is your marriage. It takes more than years; it takes a lifetime.
- No one on earth will ever know you better than your spouse, so he or she is a partner in your character development. Your spouse helps you quickly identify the chinks in your armor.

In the process of finishing well, always choose character even when it leads you down a difficult, painful or hard road. People who are constantly looking for the easy way out are not going to be shaped by or become all they're created to be.

Key No. 2: Start with the Finish in Mind

Have you ever watched a marathon? The starting line is packed with people ready to run. In some of the larger races like the Boston marathon, it looks like a sea of people. But what happens around mile 20? The sea of people becomes like droplets. The runners thin out. Those who looked fresh in the beginning now appear tired and worn out. Some walk. Some aren't even in the race anymore.

Starting something new is often easy. Anyone can start a new job or start a new project. I'm particularly guilty of this. Every time my wife, Amy, says she needs a new sandbox for our daughter, I offer to build it. After all, that's easy! I'll go down to the local hardware store and buy everything I need. But somewhere between the lumber shopping and actually hammering the first few boards, my energy wanes. I get distracted. The day ends, and the first thing the next morning, that sandbox is the last thing on my mind. Starting a project around the house is easy. Finishing it, well, that's a whole different matter.

The same can be said about our Christian journey. Choosing a relationship with Jesus Christ was the beginning of a great adventure. You couldn't help but tell your friends. You wanted to be in church every time the doors were open. You loved studying the Bible and discovering new spiritual truths and practical life applications. Prayer was easy, smooth and effortless. Over time, things changed. Bible study became more of a discipline than a delight. Distraction became the standard for your prayer life. Sleeping in on Sunday morning became all the more appealing. You may have started well, but how are you doing on the course that will eventually lead to the finish?

Being a newlywed comes easily and naturally for many couples. The passion is great and the intimacy is amazing. The relationship is blossoming. Then fast-forward 30 or 40 years. What does the couple's marriage look like now? Are they still in love? Do they still love toward each other? Have they been able to go through tough economic times, job losses, parenting, the losses of loved ones and still cherish each other?

I am so proud of and excited by couples I meet who have been married for 15, 25, 35 or 50 years. Every one of them can tell of some tough times, but they didn't allow those challenges to define their relationship; they allowed hard times to *refine* their relationship. They took what they were given or had got themselves into and grew stronger and truer to who they were called and created to be.

So how do you start with the finish in mind?

1. Foster great *conversation.* You don't want to end up like one of those couples slurping soup at Cracker Barrel. You've seen them. They can go through an entire meal with nothing to say and all you hear are the slurps.

2. Grow in *companionship.* Find things you enjoy doing together. Don't just go your own way. I know of an elderly couple in our town that gets along and has stayed married because they do nothing together. They attend different churches, sleep in separate rooms and even eat in different parts of the house. I met the husband standing outside of the movies one night and he was waiting for his wife to finish her movie. My goodness! They don't even attend the same movies together.

3. Establish *company* you both enjoy. How many times have you liked the wife but your husband did not like the husband? The other way around is often the case as well. Finding couples you click with can be tough. Think about those retirement years and all the cruises you'll go on. The company of great friends makes for a very enjoyable trip.

Amy and I learned these lessons the hard way. We now look forward to our later years in life. Enjoying dinner, conversation, friends and a distant travel destination is a great way to start with the end in mind. I think that is what Solomon meant when he said, "eat, drink and be merry. That's all we got" (the Ted paraphrase).

Key No. 3: Balance Your Attitude Between the Good and Bad Times

"Feast or famine!" That was our budgeting scenario for the first 10 years of marriage. Sometimes we had money to splurge on a vacation; but early on, we were not ashamed to have some pieces of furniture held up by egg crates. The typical start to a marriage is in the "low funds" category. When it comes to good times and bad times, I immediately think of the times of plenty and the times of want.

The apostle Paul taught that his circumstances did not determine his attitude. His attitude was centered on Christ, not his surroundings: "I am not saying this because I am in need, for I have learned to be content whatever the circumstances. I know what it is to be in need, and I know what it is to have plenty. I have learned the secret of being content in any and every situation, whether well fed or hungry, whether living in plenty or in want. I can do everything through him who gives me strength" (Phil. 4:11-13). Now that is a balanced, Christ-focused attitude!

One of the primary reasons stated for divorce is money. But we've got to tell you, money has not caused one single divorce. Money is not the root of all evil. It is the love of money (or the attitude you take about it) that is evil. Remember, when you say for richer or for poorer, your chances for starting out poorer are good.

In the Old Testament, Job had "good times." He had a family, money in the bank and his health. But in the greatest test of his life, his faith was challenged. After losing his children, his property and his health (which I would call "bad times"), his wife was done. She could not understand the test and even begged her husband to give up and die: "His wife said to him, 'Are you still holding on to your integrity? Curse God and die!' He replied, 'You are talking like a foolish woman. Shall we accept good from God, and not trouble?' In all this, Job did not sin in what he said" (Job 2:9-10).

Will your marriage balance the good times and the bad times? Will you allow trouble to bring you closer together or push you farther apart?

Key No. 4: Resolve to Stay

When we say resolve to stay, we're not talking about staying in an abusive situation. In no way are we encouraging you to stay in a relationship where there is criminal activity, physical abuse, drug abuse, habitual adultery or pornography forced upon children or spouse.

When we say resolve to stay, we're talking about the relatively trivial issues that are blamed for most divorces today. Too many couples we talk to are using wimpy reasons to try to justify divorce: "We've just grown apart"; "We don't see eye to eye anymore"; "We've lost that lovin' feeling"; "We can't get past our financial issues." Those are not reasons for divorce.

Choose your battles. Not everything needs to be a major battle. Pet peeves and annoying personality quirks are best left alone and definitely not to be harped on. Also, choose your words. Don't use the *D*-word even as part of a punch line for a joke. Don't tease with words like "my next spouse" or "trading up" or anything of the sort. And choose your audience. Live out your commitment to each other and to the marriage before your children. They need the security, especially if they have ever felt or heard the threat of divorce.

The Heart of Commitment

Dr. Scott Stanley, co-director of the Center for Marital and Family Studies at the University of Denver, provides several ideas on how to recharge your marriage and stay committed to each other. We believe his ideas will help you finish strong. Consider these five agreements you can make with your spouse to ensure your marriage lasts:

1. We agree to (increase) levels of intimacy whenever the other one so desires. We will do this by deeply listening to each other, not defending our own opinions, but striving to love, understand, and validate the other's feelings and needs.

2. We agree to highly value each other and consider each other as more important than anything else on earth, except our relationship with God. If gold could describe our honor for each other, we would each be married to a 24-carat person.

3. We agree to communicate with each other regularly. This will be accomplished by speaking to each other by sharing truthful, loving information and listening carefully to understand and validate each other's uniqueness. Our preferred method of communication will be "drive-thru listening." Drive-thru listening is the method of going back and forth until each spouse fully understands. Much like you would do at a fast food drive-thru, you repeat each other's words until "the order" is understood. Our everyday conversations will include the safety necessary to share opinions, concerns, and expectations.

4. We agree never to go to sleep at night without resolving our major differences or conflicts. We will forgive each other as

needed. Our friends Andy and Stephanie Watson have a fantastic way of resolving conflict "before the sunset." If Andy and Stephanie have a disagreement after the sun sets— which I would say is the case for most of us—they turn the lamp in their bedroom into the sun. Neither one is allowed to turn it off until they have reconciled. When I heard this, I had to ask, "How many bulbs do you guys go through in a year?"

5. We agree to find creative ways of meeting each other's deepest relational needs. As we each grow older and change, we will strive to stay current with our understanding of each other's needs, and ways of meeting those needs.[1]

In addition, we have some other recommendations for helping your marriage go the distance:

1. *Spend an evening dreaming together!* That's right, spend an entire evening making a list of activities and adventures you'd like to experience with your spouse. If you could do anything, and time and money were not factors, what would you want to do? What would your spouse want to do? Peel off the lid of reality for a few hours and dream big. Then look at the common themes and attributes of those dreams and desires. Do they include further education, travel or outdoor activities? Which dreams are mutually enriching? Are there any bite-sized pieces of the dreams that you can do in the next week, the next month or the next year? For example, if your spouse wants to sail around the world, is there a chance that he could volunteer at a local sailing club on the weekend? If you want to travel overseas, is there a place you

haven't visited within your own state that has a distinct culture or architecture? Pick several of the dreams and begin developing strategies to make them happen. When you dream together, you paint a rich picture of your lives together for years to come.

2. *Develop a plan to keep your love alive.* If you wait to feel the emotion of love, you may have to wait a long time. But if you make the decision to love, and choose to love in countless little ways every day, love can't help but come alive in your heart! What steps can you take today to help keep your love alive? What can you do to become a better listener? A better communicator? Make a list of ways you'd like to improve for each other and look for opportunities to practice them.

3. *Seek God together on a regular basis.* When was the last time you prayed, really prayed, with your spouse? Set aside time to get together on a regular basis to share what you're reading and discovering in the Bible. Look for opportunities to pray together throughout the day—while you're riding in the car, when you're taking a walk or simply sitting on the couch together.

The Beauty of Forever Together

One of my favorite textbooks in college was called *Biblical Ethics* written by one of the most brilliant theological minds of the twentieth century, Robertson McQuilken. After a long and distinguished career at Columbia Bible College (now Columbia International University), he delivered one of the most phenomenal resignation addresses I have ever heard. At the core of his resignation is his commitment to the "till death do us part" section of his wedding vows:

I haven't in my life experienced easy decision-making on major decisions, but one of the simplest and clearest I've had to make is this one, because circumstances dictated it. Muriel, now, in the last couple of months, seems to be almost happy when with me, and almost never happy when not with me. In fact, she seems to feel trapped, becomes very fearful, sometimes almost terror, and when she can't get to me there can be anger . . . she's in distress. But when I'm with her she's happy and contented, and so I must be with her at all times . . . and you can see, it's not only that I promised in sickness and in health, 'till death do us part, and I'm a man of my word. But as I have said (I don't know with this group, but I've publicly), it's the only fair thing. She sacrificed for me for forty years, to make my life possible. . . . so if I cared for her for 40 years, I'd still be in debt. However, there's much more. . . . It's not that I have to. It's that I get to. I love her very dearly, and you can tell it's not easy to talk about. She's a delight. And it's a great honor to care for such a wonderful person.[2]

Robertson McQuilken's wife lost her ability to communicate in 1995, and went to be with the Lord in 2003. For the last eight years of her life, Robertson faithfully served her with no ability to communicate with her. He's not just a hero; he's an inspiration to us all. We believe that McQuilken's story portrays something we can all aspire to in our own lives: a deeply loving relationship with our spouse. That's why in the next chapter we'll start you down that path even if your spouse isn't ready yet.

FROM GARYSMALLEY.COM

This question was sent to our website by a husband who is struggling to save his marriage.

Q: *My wife and I almost separated and divorced about two weeks ago. Thank God we decided to try to make a go of our relationship. We both love each other, but she has "closed her spirit" to me. I've tried to get her to open her spirit to me consistently for the past two weeks, using some of the techniques in the videos, but I'm frustrated by how long this is taking. I've apologized, spoken softly and spoken from my heart, but this is taking an excruciatingly long time. She says that it took a long time to get her to this point and it's going to take a long time to get her head back where it was. This is really very hurtful since I now realize how important she is to me. Is there anything I can do to speed up this process?*

A: I am so excited that you did not give up and that you are willing to give your marriage the nurturing and time it needs. The keyword is "time."

I have been married for more than 40 years. I love my wife more and more every day. You want to know something? There are days when Norma has a closed spirit toward me. You guessed it. We still must work at our marriage every day. That's what makes marriage so exciting. It is a work in progress. I am now in my sixties, but God is still working on me. He's not done with me yet.

Two keys to your success strike me as I read your email.

First, "speeding up the process" implies that you have an end in mind and that once you achieve it, all will be perfect. Don't forget, you, your wife and your marriage are a work in progress. Change is typically slow and you must allow your wife the time to heal and recover. Also, your efforts do not end when you have achieved the open spirit you desire.

Second, take this time to work on yourself. What did you do to contribute to her closed spirit? Learn from that. What is God teaching you? Learn those lessons. Take a deep look on the inside and grow each day in the power of Christ.

Trying to speed up your wife's recovery will more than likely turn out to be counterproductive. Work on the only person you can change—you! Please don't give up or lose heart. Galatians 6:9 tells us, "Let us not become weary from doing good, for at the proper time we will reap a harvest if we do not give up."

CHAPTER 11

A LAUNCHING PLACE

Jenny invited her husband to church every Sunday. When she looks back on her invites, she says it was more like throwing jabs at her husband. "The kids and I are going to church . . . when are you going to start going?"

Stephen brushed off her requests by acting busy around the house or grabbing the keys to go run errands. "It's my only day off and time to get things done," he usually replied.

Jenny got very frustrated showing up Sunday after Sunday without Stephen. "Embarrassed" is a better word to describe her feelings. People would ask about Stephen and his job out of true concern, but Jenny often felt they were saying, "You poor lady, married to a spiritually derelict man."

When I (Ted) met with Jenny, it only took one session for her to grasp the principle of personal responsibility. My challenge was simple: "Jenny, stop inviting your husband to church! Here's what I want you to do. Next Sunday, get up, get the kids ready, kiss Stephen good-bye and wish him a great morning. Better than that, invite him to meet you and the kids for lunch if he has time."

Jenny got it. This was not manipulation. It was simply backing off so God could do what only He can do—change the human heart.

Jenny embraced this approach and continued it for four consecutive weeks until she heard her husband say, "Hey, I think I'll join you guys this Sunday at church." He attended for several months before he became a follower of Jesus. I still get chills when I see God work in the hearts of people.

You do not need to wait for your mate to adjust his or her expectations or meet yours. The journey of personal responsibility starts without your mate—it actually begins with you! How do you start the journey?

Let's reflect for a moment on the progression of a healthy marriage:

The Progression of a Healthy Marriage

Unmet Expectations → Discovery → Personal Responsibility → **Commitment**

A healthy marriage is one in which you go through the stages of self-discovery and learn to identify your healthy and less-than-healthy expectations. Then you choose to take personal responsibility for your actions and reactions. Finally, you make the commitment to honor the marriage and your spouse.

In this chapter, we're going to give you three steps that lead to a healthy marriage, even if your spouse isn't walking with you yet.

Three Steps That Lead to a Healthy Relationship

If you're waiting for your spouse to change first before you take personal responsibility for what you can change in yourself, you may never see an improvement in the state of your marriage. So be the change agent in your relationship and begin showing your spouse how committed you are. Here are three ways guaranteed to improve the health of your marriage.

Step 1: Build Up Your Mate with Encouragement

I like what Mother Teresa said: "Kind words can be short and easy to speak, but their echoes are truly endless." Your spouse may feel discouraged, frustrated and tired—not just at the end of the day but every day. He or she may be going through a season in life when everything seems too hard to deal with. That's why it's so important to be a source of encouragement and hope.

Paul reminded the Thessalonians, "Therefore encourage one another and build each other up, just as in fact you are doing" (1 Thess. 5:11). He is encouraging people to watch their words, love one another and build each other up. That applies to everyday interactions, including your marriage.

My friend Scott Weatherford recently shared with me the tender story of his dad's death. His family was gathered at his bedside. On the day of his death, Scott's father asked the entire family to leave the room and come back in one at a time. As each person walked in the door, Scott's dad spoke a blessing over his or her life.

When Scott walked in the room, his father gently reminded him, "Son, you are in the second half of your life. I know that for you, the second half is going to be greater than the first half. Don't give up. Don't quit."

After Scott's father gave the last blessing, he passed away. He ended his life by encouraging his children and pouring words of hope and life into them.

What words are you pouring into your spouse? How can you bless with your words?

I (Ted) shared in our book *The Language of Sex* how Amy is crazy attracted to me when she sees me on the floor playing with our children. It is a major turn-on for her. One night she came in the family room after we put the kids down to bed and simply said, "You are a great dad!" Words of blessing do not need to be profound or long. Her statement was short and has been etched in my brain for life.

Step 2: Pray for Your Spouse

When it comes to marriage, never underestimate the power of prayer. Over the years I have literally seen hundreds of marriages on the brink of divorce come alive with joy, passion and new life because of the power of prayer.

Hebrews 4:16 instructs, "So let us come boldly to the throne of our gracious God. There we will receive his mercy, and we will find grace to help us when we need it" (*NLT*). That's right! The mercy and grace you need to love your spouse is available to you every day. Prayer is the key. Sometimes as you pray, you'll see immediate changes in your spouse; but other times the transformation will be much slower. Often when you pray, the greatest change you'll see is in yourself—in your heart, your perspective, your attitude.

Matthew 7:7-11 encourages us to be persistent:

Keep on asking, and you will receive what you ask for. Keep on seeking, and you will find. Keep on knocking, and the door will be opened to you. For everyone who asks, receives. Everyone who seeks, finds. And to everyone who knocks, the door will be opened. You parents—if your children ask for a loaf of bread, do you give them a stone instead? Or if they ask for a fish, do you give them a snake? Of course not! So if you sinful people know how to give good gifts to your children, how much more will your heavenly Father give good gifts to those who ask him (*NLT*).

That means you have the opportunity to lift the name of your spouse before God every day! It's never too late to begin praying. All too often I have found that when my emotional and relational gauges are low, and I'm low on energy when it comes to loving my wife, there's no faster way to refuel than spending time in prayer. It's hard to stay disconnected from someone you are praying for on a regular basis. In fact, it's almost impossible. You simply can't harbor anger, bitterness or frustration against someone and still ask God to bless them on a regular basis.

Imagine a six-year-old girl celebrating her birthday. Her parents sneak into her room and gently shake her awake so they can give her a present before she leaves for school. Her eyes open, but with a big yawn, she says, "Mom, since I was up so late last night, can I sleep for another hour or two? I can open my present later."

Does that ever happen? No way! The child has anticipated this moment for weeks. She's probably pulling her parents out of bed, impatient to find out what she's getting. More than likely she has been begging her mom and dad for a hint! She can hardly wait to rip off the ribbons and tear through the wrapping paper.

For me, every day is a little like a child's birthday. I try to approach God in prayer much like that six-year-old girl. I've prayed some of my prayers for years, yet each day I "get in line" with enthusiastic anticipation, asking, "Is today the day, Lord?" All day I wait to see if one or more prayers might be answered. And when they are, I often receive two packages when I only asked for one. But that only doubles the overflow, for my battery is being charged by God every day, no matter how many packages I receive—one, two or none.

Sometimes when I'm reviewing a Scripture verse, like a movie film in my mind, the lightbulb burns out or the projector malfunctions. Almost immediately a new film comes into focus, declaring that God will not be faithful to hear me again. This doubting film is so convincing that if I view it for long, I lose hope—like when I think, *There's no way God can bring joy this time.* I try to shut off the doubting film as soon as I recognize it, but sometimes it runs for several minutes no matter what I do.

Sometimes the on/off switch fails to work at all. When this happens, the only solution is to get up and walk out of the theater. Later, I reenter the theater of faith and restart the Scripture verse film. In this case, I'm big on reruns.

What is doubt? Put simply, doubt is negative faith. Doubt is allowing a film to run through our minds that says, *This will never happen to me* or *God can't do this in my life* or *I don't deserve this.* Doubt is stepping out of

God's line. Doubt is Jesus' disciples saying, *We'll never make it to the other side of the lake because of the storm.* Doubt is the widow giving up and declaring she will never receive justice. Imagine if she had gone before the judge for 100 straight days and then given up hope. She would never have known that had she persisted one more day the judge would have granted her request—just to get her out of his hair!

Step 3: Ask God to Let It Begin with You

A broken marriage begins to mend and communication is reestablished when one of the partners is willing to make a breakthrough and say, "Lord, begin with me. I am the one who needs to change, to love more deeply and more wisely."

Even if you think your spouse is 100 percent wrong, when you stand in the presence of Christ, you will begin to see that you, too, have shortcomings. You will discern where you have failed to accept responsibility for your part in the marital relationship, and you will be able to say, "God, change *me*."

A Christian should be committed to follow Christ's example. He went all the way in love, all the time. So, for a start, stop demanding that your partner change his or her ways. Let God start changing you.

Revisiting the Great Expectations Quiz

In the first chapter of this book, we asked you to take The Great Expectations Quiz. Now we'd like to challenge you to take it again and look at how your views have changed as you have gone through the material in this book.

On a scale of 1 to 10, place a number on the left side of the statement that represents what you expected in your marriage in this area. On the right side of the statement, on a scale of 1 to 10, rank what you have experienced in your marriage. For example, if you highly expected to hold hands when you were married and planned on holding hands every day for the rest of your life, give yourself a 10. But if holding hands is not a big deal, but you enjoy it from time to time, give yourself a 5. If you don't like holding hands or it's just not important to you, give yourself a 1. Keep in mind that we are looking for the gaps, because it's the gaps that cause the strain, disillusionment, frustration and hurt.

NOTE TO THOSE TAKING THE QUIZ

For those not yet married: Before you tie the knot, you need to get premarital counseling and/or training. As you talk through issues with a trusted pastor or leader, discuss your expectations honestly and openly. Use word pictures to describe what you long for, hope for and desire. Imagine a perfect day in marriage during your first year, your fifth year, your tenth year and your twentieth. Make sure you move beyond "We just love each other so much" to answering the deeper questions of the heart. Take "The Great Expectations Quiz" and share the score with your fiancé. Don't be afraid to be brutally honest—it will strengthen your relationship for the long haul.

For those already married: Now here is a caution: You may be tempted while reading this list to respond with, "Oh brother, you've got to be kidding me!" "Get over it!" or "Our puppy love went out the window a long time ago!" No matter how long ago you were married, go back to your wedding day. As you read through "The Great Expectations Quiz," what do you remember expecting on that day? What do you remember experiencing? Your marriage may be drifting . . . for some time; but what we are asking you to do is answer this simple question: Did I ever have this expectation at some point in my marriage relationship?

What you Hoped For	Expectation	What you Got
	1. We will have children. (If unable to have children, imagine the hurt and pain of a woman who wants to be a mom and her husband who wants to be a father.)	
	2. We will have many children.	
	3. We will have few children.	
	4. Long walks on the beach. (We will walk for no other purpose but connecting. Just me and my spouse, with the sand between our toes, our pants legs rolled up and the tide coming in.)	
	5. He will be a spiritual leader. (We will pray together, have daily devotions and attend church regularly.)	
	6. She will know how to submit.	
	7. Regular church attenders.	
	8. Nice house. (Imagine a white picket fence, furniture and backyard garden or downtown loft. Maybe not necessarily your first home, but your home a few years down the road.)	
	9. Romantic vacations. (Cruises, beach houses or remote cabins in the Rockies. The honeymoon experience will happen at least once a year.)	
	10. Regular vacations. (My spouse will take time away from the job or career each year to devote a full week to our marriage and family.)	

WHAT YOU HOPED FOR	EXPECTATION	WHAT YOU GOT
	11. Deep conversations. (While dating, we spent hours on the phone. There will never come a day when I sense he is "rushing" me off the phone. My spouse will always love the sound of my voice.)	
	12. Bragging on each other in public. (While dating, we talked each other up to family and friends and showed each other's picture every chance we got. This will continue throughout our marriage.)	
	13. Courtesy. (Opening doors, pushing back a chair, offering a jacket on a cold night.)	
	14. Kindness. (We will always exchange uplifting, positive words in our communication.)	
	15. Give up friends. (I know that once we get married, my spouse will no longer have a desire to spend prolonged periods of time with friends. Hanging out with me will trump hanging out with friends.)	
	16. Time with friends. (My spouse will let me enjoy plenty of time with my friends. After all, we need relationships outside of the marriage to make life rich.)	
	17. Great eye contact. (When I speak, everything will stop because what I have to say will be treasured. My spouse will remove all distractions and focus on me.)	
	18. Hand holding. (We will hold hands at all times, in the movies, in the car, at the mall, during church and even at home.)	
	19. Patience. (We will never grow tired of repeating ourselves when the other person does not understand what we are saying.)	
	20. Dress up for dates and special nights. (My spouse will always put some thought into what he/she is wearing when we date.)	

WHAT YOU HOPED FOR	EXPECTATION	WHAT YOU GOT
	21. We won't change. (Our personalities and passion will not fade or change with time.)	
	22. Dates. (From eating out to movies, we will have a regular date night that nothing interferes with.)	
	23. The "I'm glad to see you" look. (When we get home from work, there will always be an overwhelming response of elation to being in each other's presence.)	
	24. Media will not consume our time. (Our television viewing will be limited to a show/sporting event or two a week.)	
	25. Freedom from addiction. (Substance abuse, alcohol, pornography will not destroy our marriage.)	
	26. Unconditional love. (My spouse will love me even when I am going through difficult times emotionally.)	
	27. Physical health. (We will remain healthy throughout our marriage. Caring for each other through major illness will not be necessary.)	
	28. Tenderness/gentleness. (Our words will defuse anger and encourage each other.)	
	29. Validation. (My spouse will always understand my fear, frustration or hurt. Listening to me will always triumph over trying to solve my problems.)	
	30. Together forever. (We will never leave each other. The "D" word—divorce—will never be an option for us. We are together until one of us lays the other in the arms of Jesus.)	

WHAT YOU HOPED FOR	EXPECTATION	WHAT YOU GOT
	31. Snuggling on the couch. (Movie nights with popcorn will be a regular occurrence. Sometimes we will just snuggle with nothing to watch on TV. Just enjoying each other's presence will be enough.)	
	32. Sharing feelings. (I will always know my spouse's dreams, goals, hurts, hang-ups and frustrations. I will never have the need to guess, because there will always be a free flow of information.)	
	33. Grace and forgiveness. (The spirit of forgiveness will always exist in our home. We will not judge because we each are imperfect and make mistakes. There will be plenty of room for error.)	
	34. Devotions and prayer. (We will have a regular, daily quiet time with each other. We will work through the Bible, a book or devotional. We will pray at every meal.)	
	35. Cleanliness. (My spouse will always maintain a clean space, be it the closet, office, family room or bedroom. My spouse will always pick up and clean up his/her stuff.)	
	36. Closeness vs. close by. (We will always have a connectedness. We will never have the "in the same room, but checked out mentally" home.)	
	37. Humor/lightness. (We will never take ourselves too seriously. We know when to lighten up and when to laugh at ourselves.)	
	38. Servant, butler or maid. (We will cherish the opportunities to serve one another. We will always be that couple that refills an empty glass or picks up the dirty clothes of the other. Without hesitation or frustration we will look for opportunities to serve each other.)	

What you Hoped For	Expectation	What you Got
	39. Home-cooked meals. (My spouse will have the table set, dinner on the stove and even, at times, candles lit. Dinner out or ordered in will be infrequent. Meals will be as good as [or better than] my mom's.)	
	40. Understanding of work pressure. (We will work hard to give each other space at the end of a long day.)	
	41. Appreciation for work, job and career. (My spouse will show interest in what I do and what I contribute to the family's bottom line.)	
	42. Eyes for no other; faithfulness. (My spouse's "eyes" do not wander off of me and onto another.)	
	43. Ease of the words "I'm sorry." (Remember when you were first dating? When you would offend one another, not only did the apology come easily, but often it was repeated.)	
	44. Admission of mistakes. (My spouse will always be forthcoming with mistakes and character defects in his/her life.)	
	45. Appreciation for hobbies. (I will have no problem with the time required for my spouse's hobbies, and my spouse will have no problem with mine.)	
	46. Cared for when sick. (Did he or she prepare get-well baskets stuffed with tissue, soup, candles or a favorite magazine? That kindness will continue throughout our marriage.)	
	47. United front. (No one will ever be able to put me down to my mate. No parent, family member or friend would get away with slandering me to him/her.)	
	48. Protection. (My spouse will take a bullet for me if necessary. Sounds in the middle of the night will be quickly investigated and resolved.)	

WHAT YOU HOPED FOR	EXPECTATION	WHAT YOU GOT
	49. Companion. (We will love doing things together. We will never be one of those couples that go their separate way at movies, the mall or even at church.)	
	50. Sleeping together. (We will never sleep in separate rooms.)	
	51. Sex every day. (Regular sex will solve any lust problems.)	
	52. Creative sex. (Now I have the context to explore my sexual fantasies.)	
	53. Quickies. (She will serve me even when she is not in the mood.)	
	54. Sex all night. (We will make love until the sun comes up. Multiple orgasms will be experienced often.)	
	55. Family. (We will love each other's family and friends.)	
	56. Fondness of parents. (We will both get along well with our parents.)	
	57. Mom and Dad. (My spouse will like to hang around my mom and dad.)	
	58. Family history. (My spouse will show compassion for my family history.)	

WHAT YOU HOPED FOR	EXPECTATION	WHAT YOU GOT
	59. Accepting my family. (We will not judge or be critical of the actions of each other's family.)	
	60. Time with extended family. (My spouse will love spending a lot of time with my family members.)	
	61. In-law visits once or twice a year. (Mom and Dad will be able to set healthy boundaries without us needing to tell them. Visits will be minimal to help us "leave and cleave.")	
	62. Family holidays. (My spouse will have no problem with my family taking control of the holidays.)	
	63. Family traditions. (My spouse will happily honor my family traditions around the holidays.)	
	64. Decisions. (My spouse will have no problem seeing things from my point of view.)	
	65. One family income. (My spouse will make plenty of money to cover our expenses so I can stay home with the kids.)	
	66. Financial responsibility. (My mate will hold down a good job, make a good living and provide for the needs of the home.)	
	67. Financial security. (We will have plenty of money to do what we need to do as a family. We will be all about paying bills on time, keeping debt to a minimum and giving to charitable organizations.)	
	68. Financial freedom. (My spouse will have no problem spending money freely. We will not need to keep a tight rein on the checkbook.)	

WHAT YOU HOPED FOR	EXPECTATION	WHAT YOU GOT
	69. *Tithing. (We will give a minimum of 10 percent of our income to our church.)*	
	70. *Savings. (We will spend less than 100 percent of what we make so we have some to put into savings.)*	
	71. *Giving. (Money will be set aside to give to charitable organizations beyond our tithing.)*	
	72. *Retirement. (We will have plenty of money saved up so that we can stop working at a reasonable age.)*	
	73. *Church denomination. (We will mutually agree on the denomination for our family. My spouse will not bash my denominational preference.)*	
	74. *Theology. (We will merge our beliefs and have few theological differences.)*	
	75. *Worship style. (We will enjoy the same kind of worship experience.)*	
	76. *Entertainment. (From music to movies, we will be able to find a happy medium that both of us can enjoy.)*	
	77. *Promptness. (We will both work to be at events and family gatherings on time.)*	
	78. *Physically fit. (We will live healthy lives. Excessive weight gain will not occur.)*	

How have your scores changed since you first took the quiz? In what areas have you developed healthier expectations of your spouse? Of yourself? Of your marriage?

Expect Great Things from God!

We want you to finish this book with the greatest of expectations. We've talked a lot about the expectations you place on yourself, your mate and your marriage. But what about the expectations you need to place on God? Let's look at some of those expectations:

- Psalm 50:15: "And call upon me in the day of trouble; I will deliver you, and you will honor me."
- James 4:8: "Come near to God and he will come near to you."
- Psalm 32:8: "I will instruct you and teach you in the way you should go; I will counsel you and watch over you."
- John 8:12: "When Jesus spoke again to the people, he said, 'I am the light of the world. Whoever follows me will never walk in darkness, but will have the light of life.'"
- James 1:5: "If any of you lacks wisdom, he should ask God, who gives generously to all without finding fault, and it will be given to him."
- Matthew 6:14-15: "For if you forgive men when they sin against you, your heavenly Father will also forgive you. But if you do not forgive men their sins, your Father will not forgive your sins."
- 1 John 1:9: "If we confess our sins, he is faithful and just and will forgive us our sins and purify us from all unrighteousness."
- Jeremiah 29:11: "'For I know the plans I have for you,' declares the Lord, 'plans to prosper you and not to harm you, plans to give you hope and a future.'"

- Matthew 11:28: "Come to me, all you who are weary and burdened, and I will give you rest."
- Luke 6:35: "But love your enemies, do good to them, and lend to them without expecting to get anything back. Then your reward will be great, and you will be sons of the Most High, because he is kind to the ungrateful and wicked."
- James 4:10: "Humble yourselves before the Lord, and he will lift you up."
- 1 John 5:14-15: "This is the confidence we have in approaching God: that if we ask anything according to his will, he hears us. And if we know that he hears us—whatever we ask—we know that we have what we asked of him."

What a great list of promises! These promises should instill in each one of us a sense of expectation and anticipation for the abundant life we can find only through Jesus.

Say this with me aloud: "I am not God." That's why we can't fix our mate. But God can. The Bible says that God opposes the proud. What that means is that God actually stands against it. It's not that He just gets out of the way; He stands against the proud. When you say, "I can do this on my own," "I will fix this relationship," or "I will make this relationship work on my own," then you're self-dependent rather than God-dependent. James 4:6 says, "God opposes the proud but gives grace to the humble."

Embrace the grace God is offering you—grace for your life, your marriage and your future. I told Amy a few weeks ago, "Let's figure out something big that God can do through our family as we reach out to the world together!" What dreams does God want you and your spouse to live out? How does He want to use your family to accomplish His good purposes in the world around you? We invite you to dream big alongside of us and see what God can do through your healthy marriage!

FROM GARYSMALLEY.COM

This question was sent to our website by a wife who is frustrated with her husband's behavior.

Q: *I have been patient with my husband, but my patience has run out. I want to know how to keep from blasting him or wanting to instruct him on his frustrating behavior.*

A: Hide these passages in your heart:

Fire goes out for lack of fuel (Prov. 26:20, *NLT*).

He who guards his lips guards his life, but he who speaks rashly will come to ruin (Prov. 13:3).

A fool shows his annoyance at once, but a prudent man overlooks an insult (Prov. 12:16).

Don't talk too much, for it fosters sin. Be sensible and turn off the flow! (Prov. 10:19, *NLT*).

A man of knowledge uses words with restraint, and a man of understanding is even-tempered. Even a fool is thought wise if he keeps silent, and discerning if he holds his tongue (Prov. 17:27-28).

When words are many, sin is not absent, but he who holds his tongue is wise (Prov. 10:19).

The Word of God is powerful and it brings life to us. When you blast your husband, you are operating on the belief that you will get a good outcome. But do you? Does your blasting him or mothering him effect change in him?

Ask yourself this question: "What about me is bugged by my spouse?" Notice that I didn't ask, "What about your spouse bugs you?" The reason is simply because something in you needs to be examined and confessed.

Do you see how self-examination empowers you? You control how you think and react. You can't control whether anyone pushes your buttons, but you can control how you think and react to their getting pushed. If this were not the case, life would simply be an elaborate system of manipulation. But it isn't! It doesn't help a marriage to focus on all the stuff you think the other person needs to change.

My challenge to all of us in marriage is to become wordsmiths—to actually think about the words we are going to use before we speak. As you drive down the road, think about words. Guard your words; choose them very carefully; use fewer words. Don't use the same word over and over and over again.

Proverbs 16:24 tells us, "Pleasant words are a honeycomb, sweet to the soul and healing to the bones." Use the right words, loving words. Use only those words that encourage. The Bible tells us, "Do not let any unwholesome talk come out of your mouths, but only what is helpful for building others up according to their needs, that it may benefit those who listen" (Eph. 4:29).

If you watch your words and guard your heart against all manner of selfish attitudes, your marriage relationship will bring you what you've always hoped for. *Now that's an expectation based in reality!*

ENDNOTES

Chapter 1: Great Expectations
1. Some of our readers that live out West think we are crazy for making a bigger deal out of this than it really is. Keep in mind that Jon and Heather were born and raised in Southwest Missouri. We ain't got moose in these here parts. Jon and Heather did not have a clue what to do.

Chapter 2: Exposing Deep Roots
1. Wendy Pan, "Single Parent Family Statistics—Single Parents a New Trend?" *EzineArticles.com*. http://ezinearticles.com/?Single-Parent-Family-Statistics—Single-Parents-a-New-Trend? &id=1552445.
2. The suicide rate among children ages 10 to 14 has tripled in the last 10 years. Dr. Nicholi says this can be directly related to changes in the American home. One study he quoted shows that American parents spend less time with their children than parents in any other nation except England. The study quoted one Russian father who said he would not even think of spending less than two hours daily with his children. In contrast, current data indicates that the average father in the United States spends about 26 minutes each day with his children (the number drops to 16 minutes per day from children over the age of 6). See Karen Owens, PhD, *Raising Your Child's Inner Self-Esteem: The Authoritative Guide from Infancy Through the Teen Years* (Cambridge, MA: Da Capo Press, 2003), p. 312.
3. "Facts for Features," U.S. Census Bureau, 2002 data. http://www.census.gov/Press-Release/www/releases/archives/facts_for_features_special_editions/004109.html.
4. Norman Herr, PhD, "Television & Health," statistics compiled by TV-Free America. http://www.csun.edu/science/health/docs/tv&health.html#tv_stats.
5. James Jasper, *Restless Nation: Starting Over in America* (Chicago: The University of Chicago Press, 2000), p. 71.

Chapter 3: Cultural Influences
1. "Pastor Comes Clean About Porn Addiction," CBN.com, from ChristiaNet.com, June 6, 2007. http://www.cbn.com/entertainment/books/PornAddiction.aspx.

Chapter 5: Past Relationships
1. Dennis Rainey, "What Does the Bible Say About Divorce?" FamilyLife.com. http://www.familylife.com/site/apps/nl/content3.asp?c=dnJHKLNnFoG&b=3584679&ct=4639677&printmode=1.
2. Ibid.
3. Hara Marano, *D I V O R C E D? Don't Even Think of Remarrying Until You Read This*, Psychology Today, 1999, http://www.smartmarriages.com/remarrying.html.
4. Karen L. Maudlin, "*Succeeding at Second Marriages: Remarriages are more complicated and at-risk than first marriages,*" *Marriage Partnership*, Fall, 2001. http://www.christianitytoday.com/mp/2001/003/10.52.html.

Chapter 6: Expect the Best
1. "Middle C," Bible.org. http://www.bible.org/illus.php?topic_id=785.

Chapter 10: Finishing Well
1. Scott Stanley, Ph.D., *The Heart of Commitment: Cultivating Lifelong Devotion in Marriage* (Nashville, TN: Thomas Nelson, 1998), p. 215.
2. Dr. Jerry Nelson, "Husband, Love Your Wife!" sermon delivered November 23, 2003. http://www.soundliving.org/sermons/20031123.pdf.

twoignite

TWOPLAY,
TWOLAUGH,
& TWOHAVE FUN

created to strengthen marriage through action

twoignite.com

sponsored by TripFire.com

TWOPLAY, TWOLAUGH, & TWOHAVE FUN

*created to strengthen
marriage through action*

twoignite.com
sponsored by TripFire.com

Additional Resources for
As Long as We Both Shall Live

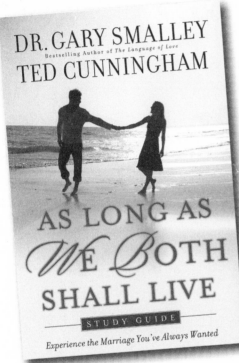

In the *As Long as We Both Shall Live Study Guide* and *As Long as We Both Shall Live* DVD, Gary Smalley and Ted Cunningham go beyond the book to dig deeper into what the Scriptures have to say about marriage and expectations. You'll find six sessions of Bible study, discussion questions and practical "next steps" to help you apply what you learn in each session. The study guide and companion DVD are fantastic resources for couples to do together, and they are equally useful for individuals, small groups, pastors and leaders.

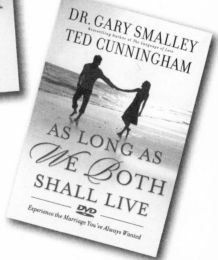

**As Long as We Both Shall Live
Study Guide**
Gary Smalley and Ted Cunningham
ISBN: 08307.46811
ISBN: 978.08307.46811

As Long as We Both Shall Live DVD
Gary Smalley and Ted Cunningham
120 minutes
ISBN: 08307.52374
ISBN: 978.08307.52379